Called to Serve

Journeys to Ordained Ministry

Called to Serve

Journeys to Ordained Ministry

METROPOLIS
OF CHICAGO

Edited by
Metropolitan Nathanael of Chicago
and
Deacon Vincent Benson

Foreward by All-Holiness
Ecumenical Patriarch Bartholomew

HOLY CROSS
ORTHODOX PRESS
Brookline, Massachusettes

Published by
Hellenic College, Inc.
Holy Cross Orthodox Press
50 Goddard Avenue
Brookline, MA 02445

ISBN: 978-1-960613-06-6

Credits: Cover art from the Samuel H. Kress Collection, National Gallery of Art
Publisher's Cataloging-in-Publication
(Provided by Cassidy Cataloguing Services, Inc.).
Names: Greek Orthodox Archdiocese of America. Greek Orthodox Metropolis of
    Chicago, author. | Symeonides, Nathanael, editor. | Benson, Vincent (David
    Richard), editor. | Bartholomew I, Ecumenical Patriarch of Constantinople,
    1940- writer of preface.
Title: Called to serve : journeys to ordained ministry / as told by the clergy of the
    Metropolis of Chicago ; edited by Nathanael Symeonides, Metropolitan of
    Chicago and Vincent Benson; preface by His All Holiness Bartholomew
    Patriarch of Constantinople.
Description: Brookline, Massachusetts : Holy Cross Orthodox Press, [2025]
Identifiers: ISBN: 978-1-960613-06-6
Subjects: LCSH: Orthodoxos Ekklesia tes Hellados--Clergy--Appointment, call,
    and election. | Orthodoxos Ekklesia tes Hellados--Clergy--Anecdotes. |
    Vocation, Ecclesiastical. | Ordination--Orthodoxos Ekklesia tes Hellados.
    | Spiritual biography. | Orthodox Eastern Church--Clergy--Appointment,
    call, and election.
Classification: LCC: BX341.5 .G74 2025 | DDC: 262/.1419--dc23

To all who have inspired, encouraged,
and prepared those who serve in ordained ministry—

To the parents and families who nurtured us,
To the teachers and mentors who formed us,
To the priests and hierarchs who guided us,
And even to those who challenged us, helping to refine and
strengthen our calling.

May this book honor your role in shaping
the clergy of today and inspiring those yet to come.

TABLE OF CONTENTS

Patriarchal Foreword   ix
Introduction   xiii

Bishop
Metropolitan Nathanael of Chicago   1

Priests
Father Tilemahos Alikakos   5
Father Richard Demetrius Andrews   7
Father Michael Arbanas   13
Father David Bissias   17
Father Stephen Bithos   23
Father Michael Condos   27
Father Michael Constantinides   31
Father Panteleimon Dalianis   33
Father Sotirios Dimitriou   37
Father Pavlos Borislav Dinkov   47
Father George Dokos   51
Father David Eynon   55
Father Panayiotis Hasiakos   59
Father Basil Hickman   65

Father David Hostetler   **69**

Father Andrew Karamitos   **75**

Father Achilles Karathanos   **79**

Father Chris Kerhulas   **87**

Father Chrysanthos Kerkeres   **89**

Father John Ketchum   **91**

Father Demetrios Kounavis   **95**

Father Nichalas March   **99**

Father Christos Mihalopoulos   **107**

Father Doug Papulis   **113**

Father Theofanis Rauch   **117**

Father Peter Sarolas   **123**

Father Dimitri Tobias   **125**

Father John Tsikalas   **133**

Deacons

Deacon Vincent Benson   **137**

Deacon Mark Bradshaw   **141**

Deacon Theodore Saclarides   **145**

Deacon Prochoros Sbarounis   **149**

Archdeacon Vasilios Smith   **151**

Deacon Paul S. Speed   **155**

Deacon Luke Twito   **159**

Afterword   **163**

PATRIARCHAL FOREWORD

Your Eminence, Metropolitan Nathanael of Chicago, beloved brother and concelebrant in the Holy Spirit, the Reverend Clergy and faithful of the Holy Metropolis of Chicago, and treasured readers of this publication, our beloved in the Lord: Grace be unto you and peace from God.

We greet you and bless the present endeavor, having been appraised of your project in which you intend to strengthen the fraternal bonds between the clergy under your pastoral care and encourage potential priests to find their calling in Christ's vineyard. This collection of essays detailing the personal journeys of the clergy of the Holy Metropolis of Chicago in their response to God's call is both timely and essential, particularly when the Church, in the United States and globally, faces the challenge of inspiring more candidates to the sacred ministry. Such efforts to cultivate unity and trust within the Body of Christ are vital to the Church's ongoing spiritual health and strength.

Thus, it is with paternal joy and honor that we offer this contribution to your work. Our own journey began on the island of Imbros, nestled in the North Aegean, where mountains rise from the shores, and countless chapels adorn the rugged landscape, offering ceaseless prayers to our merciful Lord and the Theotokos. In our home village of Hagioi Theodoroi, we were nurtured in a devout Christian family, with love, sacrifice, and service forming the pillars of our upbringing. Our parents' constant prayers and charitable deeds sowed within us the seeds of a deep commitment to Christ's Holy Church and its ministry. We saw Christ in every person and circumstance, fostering a deep commitment to serve.

The people of our treasured Imbros have always cherished education, partly inspired by the legacy of the renowned and erudite Hieromonk Bartholomew Koutloumousianos in the restoration of both secular and religious education. This love of learning shaped us from an early age. As a child, we often read when not in church, and we also helped at the olive groves or adventured through the hills. Our calling was further shaped by our father's uncle, Archimandrite Photios, and our mother's uncle, Archimandrite Joseph of the Monastery of Vatopedi. Yet, it was our village priest, the late Father Asterios, whose quiet and solemn presence first sowed the seeds of a servant's heart and a tireless spirit within us.

We often accompanied Father Asterios on foot to remote chapels for divine services. The simplicity of these services, sometimes just with the two of us, frequently held in nature, profoundly impacted us. The major feasts, such as Pascha and Christmas, were occasions of great joy. Growing older, we walked daily to the island's capital, Panaghia, to assist our spiritual father and mentor, the ever-memorable Metropolitan Meliton (Chatzis) of Imbros and Tenedos and later of Chalcedon at the eparchial headquarters. He was a living embodiment of the Church's spirit—humble yet noble, unwavering in his dedication to the sacred traditions, and deeply committed to advancing his flock.

Metropolitan Meliton strongly influenced our path to the priesthood. Under his guidance, especially after arranging for us to study at the renowned Theological School of Halki, we first felt the fruits of our calling ripen. Our time at Halki, on the "Hill of Hope," was transformative, a period marked by deep immersion in learning and prayer. On that serene island, amidst the impressive library and sacred grounds, our sense of duty, both personal and ecclesiastical, was solidified. As we wrote during our studies: "My future is full of labor and sacrifice, yet at the end, I see a hidden moral fulfillment." This awareness of duty took root at Halki and has been a guiding force throughout our life.

Following the first phase of our studies, the next step in our journey was ordination, where the calling we had felt as a child fully blossomed. Our ordination to the diaconate on Imbros was a moment of profound transformation. Metropolitan Meliton's words during that sacred occasion— "Stand with awe before the glorious light of the Transfiguration. Empty yourself, humble yourself, and make room for divine grace"—have since guided our approach to ministry, constantly reminding us of the immense responsibility we carry.

These words shaped our ministry as a deacon, and eventually, as a priest and subsequently as a hierarch.* Our time as a deacon taught us the true essence of service, a calling to assist in the Divine Liturgy, proclaim the Gospel, and serve the faithful's needs. Above all, we were reminded that we are vessels of God's grace, striving to make room for the divine in our ministry and life.

Throughout the years, we have been blessed with opportunities to travel extensively. These visits have reinforced the universality of the Church and the profound bond that unites Orthodox Christians, regardless of nationality or culture. Whether in Europe, the Americas, the Middle East, the Far East, or Australia, we have seen the same deep faith and devotion that characterize the Orthodox Christian soul.

As we reflect on our journey from our childhood in Imbros to our current responsibilities as Ecumenical Patriarch, we recall the words we wrote as a youth: "I pray that my dreams will be realized so that I may leave this world with the conviction that I have fulfilled my duties— personal, social, national, and religious." By God's grace, we have sought to live out this prayer in every aspect of our life and ministry.

We hope that through our diakonia, we have contributed in some small way to the building up of the Body of Christ and the furtherance of His Kingdom on earth. As we look to the future, we remain committed to the path set before us from our earliest days. We continue to pray for strength and wisdom to fulfill our duties, always mindful of the example set by our spiritual fathers and mentors and always seeking to follow the will of our Lord and Savior, Jesus Christ.

In closing, we offer this reflection as a testimony to the grace of God that has guided and sustained us throughout our life. We hope

---

*Note: His All-Holiness was ordained to the diaconate in 1961, receiving the name Bartholomew. In 1969, he was ordained to the priesthood, in 1973 to the episcopacy as Metropolitan of Philadelphia (Asia Minor). In 1990 he was enthroned as Elder Metropolitan of Chalcedon. On 22 October 1991, he was elected Archbishop of Constantinople, New Rome and Ecumenical Patriarch; enthroned 2 November.

these words may inspire those discerning a call to the priesthood, as well as those already engaged in ministry. We extend our heartfelt gratitude to Metropolitan Nathanael for the opportunity to share these contemplations, and we pray that the Metropolis of Chicago may continue to thrive under his pastoral care.

From our Sacred Center, we extend our paternal and Patriarchal blessing, urging you to seek moral fulfillment in the service of the Lord, striving to accomplish your duties with faith, love, and humility.

At the Ecumenical Patriarchate, December 23rd, 2024

† BARTHOLOMEW
Archbishop of Constantinople-New Rome
and Ecumenical Patriarch

INTRODUCTION

In the sacred journey of the Christian faith, the call to ordained ministry stands as a profound testament to God's divine purpose for His followers. "Called to Serve: Journeys to Ordained Ministry" is a collection of essays that delves into the personal narratives of priests and deacons who have responded to this divine call. This book not only celebrates their commitment but also offers a window into the transformative power of God's calling.

The genesis of this project emerged from my own journey as a newly appointed Metropolitan, with a desire to foster deeper connections within the clergy of the Metropolis of Chicago. Lacking extensive experience, I sought a way to build trust and camaraderie among my priests, to truly understand who they were and why they embraced ordained ministry. What began as an initiative to strengthen the clergy brotherhood evolved into a remarkable endeavor spanning four years, from conception to completion.

Through this collection, the significance of clergy sharing their stories of divine calling becomes evident. Often, priests recount their journey informally to parishioners curious about their vocation. However, there exists a paucity of written works that capture these narratives in a comprehensive manner. This book fills that gap, offering a unique written record of personal testimonies that highlight the diverse paths leading to ordained ministry.

As I continued to shepherd the Metropolis, I discovered an additional, profound purpose for this project. Beyond fostering clergy unity and mutual understanding, this book serves the faithful by allowing them to intimately know their priests. It is my fervent hope and prayer that this initiative not only strengthens the bonds among the clergy but also inspires vulnerability, trust, and a renewed sense of purpose. Moreover, I pray that it kindles the flame of vocation in the hearts of young boys, teenagers, and men who feel a special connection to God, encouraging them to pursue ordained ministry.

The role of the priest is unique, rising from the laity to serve the laity in a distinct and sacred capacity. In the words of St. John Chrysostom, a revered Father of the Church, "The work of the priesthood is done on earth, but it ranks among heavenly ordinances." This profound truth underscores the eternal significance of the priesthood, highlighting the joy and solemnity of serving God and His people.

The calling of the disciples of Christ provides a powerful example of how God calls people to serve Him and His Church. As Jesus walked by the Sea of Galilee, He saw Simon and Andrew casting a net into the sea, and He said to them, "Come, follow me, and I will make you fishers of men" (Matthew 4:19). This invitation was extended to other disciples as well, illustrating the personal and transformative nature of God's call.

It is important to recognize that this work is the first in an envisioned series of volumes on the calling to serve God. While priests are called to serve in a unique way, each baptized and chrismated individual in the Church is also called to serve God in their own distinctive manner. As it is written in the Bible, "For we are God's handiwork, created in Christ Jesus to do good works, which God prepared in advance for us to do" (Ephesians 2:10). Every person is called to become a servant of God, contributing to the divine mission through their unique gifts and callings. The next volume in this series on Divine callings will be dedicated to the special ways in which the laity serve God within the Church. It will explore the diverse and vital roles that laypeople fulfill, further illustrating the richness of God's call to His people.

I want to give special thanks to the Reverend Deacon Vincent Benson for helping take what was a concept in my mind and making it something tangible for others to enjoy. In the words of Dan Sullivan, Deacon Vincent was a special "who" in my life that helped me by lending his own gifts and talents, and filling those gaps in my own. Without his help, this book would not be possible. I also want to thank my clergy, both those who contributed to this volume and those who did not feel ready to share their calling. Each of them has been called by God to serve His holy Church, and they each do this with dignity and sacrificial love. Without them, my life has no meaning.

May this book be a source of inspiration, guiding those called to serve and enriching the spiritual lives of all who read it. May it strengthen our clergy brotherhood and inspire future generations to embrace their divine calling with joy and dedication.

St. John Chrysostom on the priesthood:

The work of the priesthood is done on earth, but it ranks among heavenly ordinances. For neither angel nor archangel nor any other created power has such a dignity as the priest who acts in the place of Christ.

— St. John Chrysostom, "On the Priesthood"

As you turn the pages of this book, may you be moved by the heartfelt stories of those who have dedicated their lives to the sacred ministry, and may their experiences inspire and uplift your faith journey.

+NATHANAEL
Metropolitan of Chicago

Metropolitan Nathanael of Chicago

In 1994, my world began to spin out of control.

I was fourteen years old when I was told Dad was diagnosed with throat cancer. He was a heavy smoker—two to three packs of cigarettes a day—so it didn't surprise anyone. We all hoped that Dad's tumor would be removed; he would go through radiation treatment; and things would go back to normal. The first two hopes came true—the third did not.

Two years after the initial diagnosis and treatment, my father's cancer returned. What was first limited to his throat now metastasized to the rest of his body. Cancer cells could now be found in his lungs, liver, and bones. Doctors gave him three to six months to live, and treatment would only extend life by a few months. Dad chose to forgo treatment. Instead, he decided to return to Greece to spend his last days surrounded by relatives and friends.

I was a sophomore in high school during this time. Suffice to say that navigating the pressures of high school was a breeze compared to grappling with my father's illness and imminent death. In May, before the end of the school year, my mother urged my sisters and me to travel to Greece to spend time with our father. His health was deteriorating quickly, and she wanted us to spend as much time with him as possible while he was still strong enough to enjoy our company. So, without knowing, I began my journey to the priesthood.

While in Greece that summer, I enjoyed many days with my father. We broke bread and laughed together; however, those summer months were quite awkward. I wasn't sure how I was supposed to behave. I was in Greece in the summer, yet I wasn't sure if I could have fun. My mother, and other adults were often very serious; they would often stop their conversation, or they would change subjects when I entered the room. My father was able to see his own mother, siblings, and other relatives and friends. He gave away all his belongings to those around him—his fishing poles, his hunting rifles, his clothes, and other possessions.

As my father's condition deteriorated, my time with him shortened. A few weeks before his passing, my mother and sisters would not let me see him too much so that I wouldn't be frightened.

Two days before his death, my father woke up troubled by a startling dream. He recounted his vivid dream to us of a large eye that gazed upon him from atop a mountain. He attempted to climb the mountain to reach the eye, and as he neared the peak, an old, bearded man in white robes struck him down with his rod. He was not allowed to approach or draw near. After several attempts, my father grew tired and gave up.

That afternoon, my father did something that surprised us all— he asked to see a priest. We were all dumfounded. Dad was not a churchgoer. By modern standards, he not only wasn't religious," he also wasn't "spiritual." Naturally, my father was baptized an Orthodox Christian as an infant, but he never lived his faith. So, for him to ask for a priest caught us all off guard.

After spending some time with Dad, the village priest told my family that Dad had just received the Sacraments of Reconciliation (Confession) and Communion (Eucharist). The next day, he died peacefully.

For years following that summer, I struggled to understand my father's last acts. Why on earth did my father, who rarely attended church services—not even on Christmas or Pascha—end his life by entering sacramental unity with Christ? It would take three years for me to discover the answer.

As a nineteen-year-old college freshman, I recall being invited by my parish priest to serve as a counselor during winter camp. At the time, his invitation meant little more than a free ski weekend in New England; I couldn't wait to hit the slopes! Boy was I wrong.

One evening, my priest announced to the campers that the Sacrament of Confession would be offered the next morning. Confession, I thought. That's what Dad did before he died! I don't think I went to sleep that night. Should I go to confession? Was this for me? What would I confess? How would my priest react to what he heard? These are just some of the questions that went through my mind.

Early that morning, my priest found me standing outside the doors of the chapel. He asked me what I was doing there so early. I told him I wanted to go to confession. We walked into the chapel and proceeded with the sacrament. Confessing my sins for the first time as a young adult not only gave me great inner peace and joy, but it also eased my heart, reassuring me that my father was in God's hands. My struggle to understand the last actions of my father would be quieted. I realized then and there what a blessing it was for my father to end his life in such a blessed state.

From that moment, I longed to serve others, to serve as God's instrument of His peace, mercy, and love. I realized that I was called to serve as a priest of the Most-High God.

His Eminence Nathanael (Symeonides) is the Metropolitan of Chicago, which is comprised of 58 parishes and two monastic communities in Illinois, Indiana, Iowa, Minnesota, Missouri, and Wisconsin.

Father Tilemahos Alikakos

M y first childhood priest was Fr. Konstantinos Orfanakos who served the parish of Saint Nicholas in Sparta, Greece. The church was under construction at that time, and the services took place in the church basement which was dedicated to the Three Hierarchs. I was just under six years old when Father Kosta invited me to serve in the altar during the Divine Liturgy. By the end of that service, I knew I was home.

I continued serving in the altar with Fr. Konstantino and getting involved in the life of the parish through sports, theater, and small youth groups. I also had the chance to go to catechism class on Saturdays with Fr. Dionysios, who was a celibate priest and former missionary to the Congo. He also led summer camps at Holy Anargyroi monastery, located about thirty minutes from the town, and he had a great influence on me as my first father confessor and mentor.

The good thing about growing up in a small town like Sparta was that I could walk to church whenever I wanted, which made it easier to fill the years of my youth with great experiences around parish life. However, all that changed when at the age of 14, my family and I returned to Chicago. It took a while for me to find my bearings, but at least the church part was settled nicely when I found a home at Holy Taxiarhai and Saint Haralambos in Niles, Illinois. With the blessings of the parish priest, Fr. Dean Botsis, I started serving at the chanting stand and found myself immersed in a brand-new church family.

Throughout this time, thoughts of committing to a life in the priesthood always circled in my mind. It seemed, however, a difficult path to take and truly overwhelming. I was doing well at school and was expected to become an engineer, a professor, or a scientist. I pursued a degree in mathematics and statistics while continuing to postpone thoughts about the priesthood.

During my undergraduate studies at Loyola, I took a class on Orthodoxy, taught by Father Nikitas Lulias (currently the Archbishop Thyateira and Great Britain). After the class was over, we kept in touch and he knew that upon graduation from Loyola, I was poised to continue to graduate studies at Northwestern in statistics and actuarial sciences. Nevertheless, that July of 1994, Fr. Nikitas invited me to his office at St. Demetrios in Chicago and told me that I had to change course and enroll at the seminary. Somehow, he knew that a life in the church was always my dream even though the life of the priesthood terrified me. With his prayers and guidance, and with the blessing of Fr. Dean, my parish priest, I applied to Holy Cross and enrolled at seminary with the hope and prayer that this was indeed what God wanted from my life.

Father Tilemahos Alikakos serves at Holy Taxiarhai and Saint Haralambos Church in Niles, Illinois.

I've told this story, or at least parts of it, many times, but I've never written it down. It's difficult to say exactly, but the seeds of calling to the priesthood could have been planted when I was a young child. My mother, Maria, was born in Crete (1943) and immigrated as an eight-year-old child (1951) with her family to La Crosse, Wisconsin. As a teenager and young adult, she became disconnected from the Greek Orthodox Church. Around this time, she met and married my father (Richard Vernon Haugen) in a Lutheran church in Minneapolis but divorced three years later. Soon thereafter, she met my stepfather, James Marshall Andrews (a South Dakota native). Seeking to reconnect with the faith of her upbringing, Mom married Jim at St Mary's Greek Orthodox Church (1968), and he legally adopted me the same year. My name was changed to Richard Demetrius Andrews, my new middle name an ode to my new father and my Mom's Greek heritage. I have very faint memories of the wedding ceremony.

Within a few months, we moved to Sioux Falls, South Dakota (1969), but I don't really remember Holy Transfiguration Church, nor the priest's son, even though we had a few play dates. After a brief return to Minneapolis, my dad took a new job with First National Bank, and our family moved to Great Falls, Montana, where we lived for the next seven years (1970-1977). I do have memories of the little Greek Orthodox church there, probably because my parents befriended the priest and his family who recently immigrated from Greece and spoke no English. There is a great photo of me, my dad, and the priest sitting at our dining room table when I was five years old. During this time, we also attended the Congregational (Protestant) church because that was my dad's faith tradition, and they had a large, active youth program (the Greek Orthodox parish was too small for this). My first summer camp experience was in 1976 at Camp Mimanagish in the mountains of south-central Montana.

In 1977, my dad's work took us back to Minneapolis. Immediately, we immersed ourselves in parish life at St Mary's Greek Orthodox Church. My parents brought me to Divine Liturgy, Sunday church school, and youth group every week, along with yearly summer church camp and basketball tournaments. This spiritual routine continued through junior high and high school. My senior year was a whirlwind of sports (football), academics (National Honor Society, Salutatorian) and partying, but deep inside, subconsciously I knew something was missing.

The summer after I graduated (1982) I traveled with 20 other teenage friends from church to the Patriarch Athenagoras Retreat Center (PANRC) in the foothills outside of Cheyenne, Wyoming. The weeklong camp program was a profound experience, not only because it was my first trip back to the mountains since we moved from Montana five years earlier, but also because I experienced Christ in powerful ways. Many of the male staff were seminarians at Holy Cross Greek Orthodox School of Theology in Brookline, Massachusetts. I sensed in them something I was missing in myself. I saw my current friendships in a new light, and during the camp, we made fast friends with another group of campers from Milwaukee, Wisconsin.

Sometime during that week, I had a conversation with the camp director, Mr. George Pyle (several years later in 1992 he would become youth director at my current parish of Saints Peter and Paul in Glenview Illinois and was ordained a priest in 1997). He asked me if I ever thought about being a father. I casually shrugged and said, "I dunno, I suppose I'll get married and have kids someday." He replied, "No, I mean have you ever thought about becoming a priest?" I dismissively retorted, "No," looking like, "what a stupid question." He calmly responded, "Well, I think you should because you'd be good at it." I thought he probably said that to all the young men who attended camp at PANRC.

I didn't give a conscious second thought to Mr. Pyle's question, but he and the retreat center experience made a huge impact on me. I had a rocky college experience, making it through two years of engineering school before quitting to work full-time for a couple years. During that time, I reconnected with my birth father. I returned to PANRC three separate summers, each time with a smaller and smaller group, but I had deeply enriching and fulfilling spiritual experiences. I finally resumed my university schooling, changing my major to business administration and marketing.

As I neared graduation, I started thinking very intently about a career and what type of job I would like to do and be good at. I received invaluable help and wise guidance from so many people during high school and college including our youth directors, Elaine Makres (who is now Mother Macrina of Holy Dormition Monastery in Rives Junction, Michigan), Harry "Bumper" Boosalis (who went on to teach theology for 25 years as a professor at St Tikhon Seminary in Pennsylvania), and Hans & Sue Jacobse (one of the most intellectually and spiritually gifted people I have ever known. Fr. Hans went on to serve parishes in Greek and Antiochian Archdioceses).

Because I had been helped by so many, I had an inkling that I wanted to work in a job where I could also help others. Because of my business major, I started looking at careers in personnel and human resources. However, as I learned through some informational interviews, those jobs were still subservient to a corporate agenda. Thus, I began to seriously consider a career in psychology or psychiatry. Yet, at that time, people in those disciplines were often indifferent or hostile to religion and spirituality. I felt like I was reaching a dead-end and not sure where to turn.

Around this time (1989), I worked as a counselor at St. Mary's Summer Church Camp in Minnesota, the same camp I attended as a teenager from 1977-1981. The first night, we were in the chapel after the evening worship service, and I noticed a man enter. He seemed out of place because he was wearing Bermuda shorts, high top tennis shoes, a tank-top t-shirt, and a baseball cap on backwards along with dark sunglasses. I thought, this guy must have taken a wrong turn off the road to end up in our secluded campsite in northern Minnesota.

As it turned out, this man was our priest for the week. We quickly became acquainted that week, and I came to know Fr. Nick Kasemeotes as a priest who was fully himself in his priesthood. He didn't give the impression that he was trying to be someone else or what others thought a priest should be. At the end of the week, a light bulb went on in my mind—a deep voice within told me to go to seminary to help people grow in their faith. It was like the fog of the past several years had cleared and I finally had my powerful purpose.

In retrospect, I believe the seed of God's calling to ministry was planted seven years prior, during my brief conversation with George Pyle. I realized the soil of my heart had been tilled previously through years of church-centered experiences and friendships. I realized that a darker part of my upbringing along with sinful choices during my teenage and young adult years had hardened my heart, created a lot of inner turmoil, and darkened my ability to see my true self.

I realized that, in the back of mind, I had been thinking of the priesthood. but could never picture myself as a priest because I thought I was not worthy. Even if I was, I had to be like the other priests I knew growing up, especially my parish priest, Fr. Anthony Coniaris. Fr Anthony was a great priest, a prolific writer and preacher but also an extremely shy, reserved, and strait-laced person. At the time, I just could not relate to that, although in some ways I had similar personality traits.

Once I met Fr. Nick, that barrier was removed and I subsequently shared with him, "If you can be a priest, then anyone can be a priest." I was sincere and well-intentioned in my sentiment, even though it sounded somewhat condescending. I was also excited about my new-found purpose and began to share it with close friends, including my girlfriend at the time, Jane. Everyone was very affirming, and I think many already knew what I had just discovered. What seemed like such a treacherous uphill battle beforehand, after my light-bulb moment became like coasting downhill as everything started falling into place.

In retrospect, God closed doors to guide me in a certain direction, and now He was opening doors with symbolical signs saying, "Go this way!"

In September, I visited the two major seminaries at the time, first St Vladimir's in New York and then Holy Cross in Brookline. Holy Cross was the easy choice because of the familiar and family-like atmosphere. I knew many of the seminarians from my trips to Wyoming several years before. In October, I asked Jane to marry me. In November I started working full-time at Light & Life Publishing, Fr Coniaris' book distribution business. Three months after our wedding in May 1990, Jane and I packed a small moving truck full of our furniture and belongings and moved to Brookline.

There are many more details and stories, but these are the major events of my journey of being "Called to Serve."

Father Richard Demetrios Andrews serves
at Saints Peter and Paul Church in Glenview, Illinois

Father Michael Arbanas

It seemed like a natural move: after nine years as a newspaper reporter, I'd go to the seminary and eventually become a parish priest.

At least, it seemed natural to me. Not so much to my colleagues, family, or friends, though.

Most of my co-workers in the newsroom knew I went to church regularly, and that was puzzling enough; leaving for the seminary was downright mystifying. My girlfriend, Caroline (who is now my wife), would suggest that I was simply having a bad day whenever I brought up the subject, and my mother actually enlisted friends and relatives to call me – even after I had quit my job and was traveling to the seminary – and try to talk me into going to medical school, law school or anywhere else.

I certainly understood why it might seem like a big leap. Once in a used bookstore, I spotted a slim volume called The Christian

Journalist. I regret that I didn't buy it, and I can't remember the author's name. However, I do recall a sentence from the introduction that said something like, "The idea of a Christian journalist may seem like an oxymoron; after all, the newsroom is a place where the Lord's name is rarely spoken, unless it's taken in vain."

However, I didn't feel the inconsistency, and I knew I wasn't the only one. For example, James Scudder, a tremendous reporter who sat at the desk right across from mine at the Arkansas Gazette, was a part-time pastor at a small-town Methodist church, about forty-five minutes from Little Rock. Another editor in the features section was also a Methodist minister. A life of faith wasn't quite as inconsistent with the vocation of reporter as one would think.

Despite this, I never really discussed the call to ministry with those colleagues. After Little Rock, I worked at newspapers in Boise, Idaho, and Mobile, Alabama, working with other men and women of faith, before finally deciding to explore what it would mean for me to serve the Gospel of Jesus Christ.

When people would ask why I was making the change, I would deflect with humor: "I'm looking for a job where I only have to work one day a week," or something like that. The truth is that I had a number of inter-related motivations – some of them positive and others negative – that pushed me toward the seminary.

I attended a Roman Catholic high school and was one of a handful of boys who paid attention and participated during the vocations retreat that all seniors had to attend. However, I also had other ideas and ambitions, and I wasn't ready to make any kind of commitment to serve. It just went to the back of my mind.

I was definitely influenced by the social justice teaching that was a part of the curriculum in the late 1970s, and this inclination only grew in college when I was exposed to the work of Dorothy Day and the Catholic Worker movement. Much of it resonated with what I was hearing in the Orthodox Church, especially in the Gospel readings. Ever since, I've appreciated the experience of being challenged and even humbled, especially by the Gospel.

I graduated from Wayne State University in my native Detroit with ambitions to be creative in music or literature, but with no clear direction. Eventually, I ended up studying journalism, first at Wayne

State and then at Columbia University. I could write well, and here was a way to make a living, so I pursued it.

Aside from the practicality, I was convinced that I could make a positive contribution to society through journalism. Democracy, after all, functions best when people make informed decisions as they vote.

Likewise, getting the best, most complete information about any subject can help people overcome prejudice, animosity, and fear – making them better citizens and better people.

This may seem to be an overly idealistic view, but I actually saw it at work. The Arkansas Gazette, where I got my first reporting job in 1987, was a positive force in the state throughout the Little Rock school-desegregation crisis in 1957 and ever since. The Gazette hadn't eliminated racism or backward thinking in the state, but it had earned the trust of a lot of people that it would not pander to them, but rather give them the information they needed to make good decisions and develop better-informed opinions.

The Gazette closed in 1991, and although I later worked with some wonderful people at the newspapers in Boise and Mobile, I was becoming restless. I was less and less interested in the indirect approach of providing information to large groups of readers, and I was increasingly drawn to the idea of becoming involved in the lives of individuals and families – as Jesus did in the Gospels.

This impulse gelled in me when my best friend got married, and I stood up in the wedding. I remember distinctly thinking about the priest – a rather quirky fellow whose hobby was skydiving – and what a privilege it would be to be involved in the important passages of people's lives like weddings, baptisms, and funerals. Pondering this, it all came together for me.

By studying, I would understand the Gospel better and could share it with others in ways that challenged their thinking and helped them grow into more loving, merciful, and kind people. I might not be reaching tens of thousands of newspaper readers, but I'd have direct contact with parishioners, week afyer week, and I'd also have the blessing of walking with them through good times and difficult times So, it did make sense.

I didn't decide right away, though. I made some inquiries with my parish priest. "You're in luck," he said. "The bishop will be in town Friday, and you can talk with him, too!" So, I spoke with our bishop, much sooner than I had anticipated. I contacted the seminary. I thought and prayed about it.

I talked with Caroline. We had been carrying on a long-distance romance for four years, and it wasn't easy. As I had been speaking with the bishop, I was struck by the thought: "I can't make this decision on my own; we have to make it together." This was followed by another thought: "Wait. That's how married people think," and that's when I decided to propose to her. First, we talked about the seminary and the priesthood. All kidding about having a bad day aside, she had become increasingly aware that studying at the seminary and exploring the possibility of serving in the priesthood was important to me, and she was willing to be a part of it. We were married the summer after my first year at school.

The nine years I spent as a reporter were very helpful in my studies and my ministry. Reading complicated legal filings and legislative bills to discover what about them was important helped prepare me to zero-in on the main points of the sometimes expansive (to put it mildly) works of theology that were part of the coursework. Reporting for a general audience also helped me learn to write clearly.

Reporters sometimes find themselves in very uncomfortable conversations, which is good preparation for being with people in sad, difficult situations, without running away. After all, if I'm preaching about our God who doesn't abandon His people, the least I can do is stick with them when they're struggling, as uncomfortable as it may be.

I was thirty-three years old when I entered the seminary. My newspaper reporting was an important preparation for my studies and work. Of course, there are plenty of areas I find to be challenging too. Everyone has their strengths and what kind people and human-resources officers might call "opportunities for growth." In other words, nobody's perfect.

There's nothing in the Holy Scriptures that speaks of perfection as a pre-requisite for serving the Lord. The main requirement is love – for God and for our neighbors, whoever they might be. As St. Paul said to the Romans, "Having gifts that differ according to the grace given to us, let us use them" (Rom. 12:6).

*Father Michael Arbanas serves at
Saint Nicholas Church in St. Louis, Missouri.*

Father David Bissias

As a young child I ditched Sunday school frequently. In fact, I have very few clear memories of actually attending Sunday school at all. Whenever the opportunity arose—perhaps the teacher stepped out of the room momentarily, or I asked to use the boy's room (whether necessary or not) — I would ditch.

The main problem for me was that Sunday school was held during Divine Liturgy ("for adults" we were told). Between Matins and the Divine Liturgy, the parish priest would conduct a brief service for the students and staff, consisting of some recited prayers and hymns. I actually liked this brief ceremony. I learned to sing the hymns in English and Greek—though the latter was still a very foreign tongue to most of us. I begged my mother to get us there early, not because I wanted a good seat in the front as I usually had, but because if I was lucky, I was able to see the end of Matins, and a few times I was early enough to see the priest offering incense throughout the church and narthex, vestments flowing behind him. I could listen to the chanter and the priest singing words I did not understand, but the melody and deep voices enchanted me. Together with the smell of lingering incense, and the early morning light shining onto the gold mosaic icons and the large blue apse with the gigantic icon of the Theotokos holding the infant Jesus, I was in a new, impressive, world.

At the end of the service, we would file past the priest, kiss his hand, and receive the blessed bread (antidoron), and go with our teachers to class. More often than not, during this march to class, I would plan my escape.

I had only one destination: to re-enter the church during the Divine Liturgy. I would slink through a side door into the nave and stealthily (so I believed) tiptoe over the front-center pew occupied for years by my great-aunt, and then stand attentively next to her. She invariably would look down at me and smile, then seemingly pretend I was not there. Early on, my teacher would find me and, with an exasperated look, seek to bring me back. At first, I would, not able to defy an adult. Then one Sunday after a few repetitions of this ritual, my great-aunt said something in my defense.

"Leave the child." She said it quietly but without even looking at the teacher or at me. She just put her left hand on my shoulder and made the sign of the cross with her right in response to whatever was occurring in the service. The teacher was unable to argue.

Standing next to my great-aunt, I went to work. I remember consciously mimicking the actions of the priest when he faced us. I eagerly anticipated the processions with the altar boys and their near-military precision. I would escort my great-aunt (or she escorted me) when it was time for Holy Communion. She always asked me if I wanted to receive. I always did. She then always asked if I had eaten anything. I always said no (which was not always true, I confess). I always went up and said my name. The priest always gave me a curious look as if my presence was most unexpected. Except for infants, it seemed that I was usually the only youngster in line. Occasionally, Sunday school students would come at the end.

I do not recall a time in my childhood when I did not want to be a priest. Indeed, in my tender years while other neighborhood friends wanted to play "cops and robbers" or pretend to be soldiers, cowboys or Indians, I would play priest. A blanket served as my vestment. A string of small cowbells, my censor. I sang the few short hymns I knew, over and over. My hardcover, illustrated children's Bible was placed on my altar, the couch. Once I could read, at a rather young age, I used a small service book to recite some of the prayers. I would hush anyone in the house making noise. I did try to maintain some standard of reverence!

Family members were well aware of the "strange" nature of my play, but certainly did nothing to discourage it. In fact, my godfather (nouno) recorded a recitation of the Nicene-Constantinopolitan Creed for me so I could learn it in the original language. At least for a few years, I was always certain that I would grow up to be a priest. I never questioned it; I never doubted it. It just seemed what I was to do.

In my adolescence, however, some things changed. When talk arose among my friends about what we wanted to do with our lives, I switched to "lawyer." I don't know why I chose that occupation—it wasn't the truth—but I am certain that "priest" would not have been considered cool among my peers.

Furthermore, although admiring him from a distance, I was never close to my parish priest, and recall no lengthy conversation with him prior to attending seminary. Frankly, though I continue to admire and respect deeply his work and ministry today (may his memory be eternal!), he was not particularly close to any of the kids in my age group. So as a young person, the priest was, for me, primarily the liturgical celebrant. Impressive as he was in the role, I had no real personal relationship with him.

This changed around the time I could drive myself to church as a teenager. Some relatives introduced me to their parish priest at a family party. He was truly inspirational and engaging. Through my cousins' teasing, he learned of my early attachment to the services—skipping Sunday school in favor of liturgy, playing "priest"—and invited me to come to serve in the holy altar at his church—which I did. My first conversation with him was the longest I had ever spoken to a priest, and it was as if he was a normal person!

Soon, that priest became, for me, a mentor, friend, and guide. Learning of my interest in music, he shared his own history as a teen in a moderately successful rock band, and he encouraged me to learn the Byzantine music of the services and taught me all I ever needed to know about the liturgical services. He let me tag along with him during breaks from school to assist at house blessings and other occasional services. He gave me every opportunity to see, in person, the daily life of a priest, including those times when he would visit socially with his friends among the clergy. Though he never pushed the idea, he always encouraged me to attend seminary. In the truest sense, he became my spiritual father, long before I knew the phrase. I truly believe that if it were not for meeting him and his encouragement, I may have veered from the path I started on from my earliest days.

All this is to explain my own sense of calling—or lack of a specific "calling" in terms of some interior voice or a particular moment or catalyst—and an inclination to serve the church from my youth. Yet when I was in seminary, and for some time thereafter, I have considered what was instilled within me to follow that path.

First, the earliest but perhaps least important factor, was the aesthetic attraction. I vividly recall as a youngster the effect everything about our liturgical tradition had on my senses of sight, hearing, taste and smell. From early on I had a love for making music and singing, and the Church's musical tradition was fascinating to me. Likewise, the forms and styles of iconography instantly appealed to me. I may have been unable to articulate it at the time, but the Church did make present to me a different and special world.

Second is what I call a gift for performance: I have always been comfortable speaking, singing, or performing publicly. I was never reticent to interact socially on any level, even to the point of precociousness as a child. I always wanted to be engaged with others in conversation or common cause. Though this could have led me in different directions, being a chanter or priest was attractive because of all they able to do at the services.

Third, and most important to me, but certainly harder to explain, is a profound sense of gratitude. Realizing this has taken me many years, because it goes far beyond describing myself being thankful to God and returning God's favor by my own service. That is too simple, for it is not as if I consciously thought to myself as a child that I was grateful to God, thus I would serve as a priest. I will try to express this sense of gratitude in the manner it came to me, which was over many years.

My gratitude is directly related to the fact that I was adopted. This is where things get complicated.

I was born into the world and then taken home from the hospital by my adoptive parents. I have always known; my parents were always open about it. My godmother, from when I was a very young child, always reminded me of how special I was because I was chosen. A part of me was always proud about that, in a positive way. I felt loved in a special manner because I was adopted, though I recognize that among adopted children this is not always true. I was not, however, a perfect child. My father once told me, "I don't care what you do, or who you do it with, but you have my name. Understood?" It was. It was my father's way of letting me know boundaries, and that he expected I would not bring shame on myself or, by extension, to him. It was a lesson from my early adolescence that has stuck with me. I did not see it in the negative manner by which he may have meant it (as if he meant, "don't do anything to embarrass me"); I always wanted to honor him, and my mother, by making them proud. While sometimes slow to appreciate it, from my teens I was very aware of the sacrifices and struggles of my father to support, defend, and provide for his family, and the satisfaction and happiness—because of the sacrifices and struggles— this brought him.

I was "adopted" as well by my spiritual father, and this led to my sense of belonging to the wider community of faith, a communion, literally a "shared existence." His welcome and encouragement led to my being involved in the church which became, in some sense, my home away from home, for which I was thankful. His "adoption" of me led to a whole new social setting, an extension of what family meant, and the members of this network were dedicated to serving the church in some manner. I was able to see him ministering and the joy and happiness — not without sacrifice and struggle — this brought him.

It was my spiritual father who, upon learning of my adoption from birth, pointed out the theological importance of our adoption in Christ by our Heavenly Father. Over many years, I have reflected on this through the lens of my own experience: how out of gratitude I wanted to honor my own father, how I wanted to emulate my spiritual father. I learned very early on that "blood ties" were not the only, or even best, basis for love and commitment. I wanted to be worthy of my own father's name, and then realized I needed to strive to be worthy of the Name above all names!

I was adopted, and I was grateful.

So, when asked by persons why I chose to become a priest, I find it rather hard to answer. I do not recall making a conscious choice. In fact, the only choice I am conscious of was one to reject being a priest.

I was born, and I was adopted (thrice, as the service books would describe it), and all the innate skills and talents granted me, instilled in me, and taught to me by my father, by my spiritual father, and by my Heavenly Father, presented me a path that, out of gratitude, I followed. It led me to my ministry within the Body of Christ, for which I am always thankful.

Father David Bissias serves at
Saint Demetrios Church in Hammond, Indiana.

Father Stephen Bithos

Reflecting upon life at this point in time opens my mind to the realization that every experience, whether positive or negative, has been a most valuable and beneficial tool in molding my character and understanding of my life's purpose.

The decision to enter the priesthood was not the course that I had desired. Growing up in a home with a father who was a priest and other relatives who had entered into the service of our Lord, it may have seemed natural to others that I would follow in the footsteps of our family members. But that was not the case. My intent was to enter law school. The two schools of law I had applied to had accepted my entrance, and the choice was made. I was to begin classes on my return from a short vacation in Greece.

Being present in Greece, I was overwhelmed by the beauty in the country of my ancestors and of the ever-surrounding presence of our Orthodox Faith. Gradually I came to the realization that I wanted the daily life of serving the church in some capacity, but the idea of the priesthood was still not the avenue I thought of pursuing. At that time circumstances halfway through my vacation, along with family difficulties, prohibited my mind from allowing my heart to open its doors to the path of the priesthood.

Fortunately, I was blessed to have a spiritual relationship with a respected hierarch of the church, who took me under his protection while I was in Greece. It was through his guidance and prayers that I was able to come to the understanding that my love of faith and the belief that God had called me to cooperate trustingly with his plan was the path I could not avoid. Even though the full scope of that plan remained a complete and utter mystery to me, and even though he often left me shaking my head in wonder. I eventually came to realize in a new way that God asked that I allow myself to be moved both figuratively and literally by his will, that I learn to float easily on the tides of his providence, and that I cast objections and second-guessing aside and simply say: "Yes, I hope and pray that the lesson will sink in deeply and thoroughly."

Another aspect that led me to accept the calling of our Lord was when I took the time to delve into the scriptures. I was struck by the determination, courage, humility, and most especially, the Lord's love for his flock. I thought; without such love, how could he have endured the passion and all it entailed? I realized that from God's perspective, we are the pearl of great price, the buried treasure, the lost coin, the lost sheep, the lost son, the unforgiving ones with the unpayable debt. We must mean much more to him than we imagine, that he would give his Son for us, stingy as we are with our love and fickle in our faithfulness. So, with all this in mind, I started to think about the passion of Christ. In my mind I found myself taking the part of the crowd, too, because I realized that I am one of those for whom he paid the ransom. I am one of the ungrateful ones, one of those whose flesh tires and fails to keep watch with him. So now I speak the words of Jesus since I am called by him to be his priest and to love his flock and in my heart, I know that I am as indebted to him as anyone else, and probably more.

So, with all my thoughts on the gradual change that took part in my life, I had come to the conclusion that a conversion took place in my heart. There was no sudden eureka moment. No visitation of Jesus or the Panagia. No angels coming to enlighten me. It was merely a conversion that took place. This conversion brought peace to me. This conversion brought my life into sync with my purpose and destiny. Therefore, I believe that conversion is also a critical part of the witness we as priests are to give to those we serve: we are to be signs of hope who strongly trust in God's transforming power and seek each day to be even clearer signs of the kingdom.

On the one hand, I am humbled and comforted that Christ works in me despite my unworthiness and ineptitude. On the other hand, I see clearly that the indelible sacramental character of ordination is at the same time a call to conversion and personal holiness – so that by his grace there will be less and less a discrepancy between who I am and how I act. The means to answering that call is prayer. Through prayer, God breathes the kingdom into me deeper and deeper, without my even knowing it.

Accepting a life of spiritual influence has been a freeing experience of life, it has confirmed that God has called me to be a priest and to be a part of the lives of others, hopefully in a spiritually uplifting and holy manner.

This calling has instilled within me the unwavering witness to the importance of being faithful to prayer.

We must be open to the Lord's call wherever and whenever that may be. The Lord will never let us be more generous to Him than He is to us. I have found that God's will is found in the voice of the Church, especially if I would rather be left alone. Each of us is asked to carry our cross which is as different for each of us as we are different from one another. It is in the carrying of that cross that we find our salvation. Because our God is a God called LOVE, we can do nothing better in our lives than love. I have found that it is so very important to have a special love for all those within the church.

I have been pondering my response to invitations from God to place myself at his disposal in the seemingly routine events of every day. Situations I have faced thousands of times before – passing a stranger on the street, attending a meeting, returning a phone call, preparing a sermon, visiting the hospital – might be the moment God will use to make himself known to him or her. Therefore, every moment of each day is an opportunity to grow, reflect and serve Christ in a unique way. It is the path I have traveled for the last forty years and there are no regrets to the decision I made so many years ago.

Glory be to God for all things!

Father Stephen fell asleep in the Lord while serving St. Nicholas Church, Oak Lawn on January 25, 2024.

Father Michael Condos

I recall, many years ago, on a sunny and hot late summer day, taking my first steps onto our seminary campus. It was, in one manner, exciting, and in another, overwhelming. I began to question myself. "Was I truly called to serve the Lord as a priest? Would I be able to learn all that would be required of me? Did I do the right thing moving to Boston?"

During one of our orientation sessions, one of the priest-professors, Fr. Stanley Harakas (now of blessed memory) seemed to anticipate these questions. As our small band of brothers sat, huddled together in the beautiful chapel, beholding the holy icons gleaming with a single ray of sunlight, Father addressed these questions, describing two things that were of utmost importance when considering a call to serve as a priest. They are: 1) an inclination and 2) a call from God.

As Father spoke, my eyes turned towards the icon of our Lord. I began to reflect upon whether or not I truly had that inclination. Then, it was as if our Lord returned me to my childhood. I began to recall the way my mother read the Scriptures to my brother and me from a very young age. It was my mother who taught us to pray. She took me to the church for my first confession at age seven. She guided me, although herself a convert to Orthodoxy, through the Divine Liturgy, which was celebrated solely in the Greek language. As I grew older, she led me to serve in the altar as an acolyte. Even when I was not "on duty," if she would see the priest by himself at the Holy Altar, she would tell me to go inside to "ask Father if he needs help."

She also placed my brother and me in a parochial school for several years, until I entered high school. It was there that I was able to freely discuss religion, ask questions, and come to appreciate the Orthodox Christian faith in a deeper manner. As these memories passed before my mind's eye, I came to understand that I did, in fact, have the inclination to serve as a priest.

After high school, I believe this inclination was leading me to desire to serve in the military. I wanted to enlist in the Navy. I also applied for a scholarship to college through the Reserve Officer Training Corps. I had even considered going to school to become a policeman. I recall speaking with an older priest who told me that quite often a call to serve Christ as a priest is mistaken for some other type of civil or military service.

I decided, after graduation, to enroll at Indiana University. After a year of studying and, without a clear desire to pursue a specific field of study, my father suggested that I follow him into a career in insurance marketing, which I did. I would go on to work in the insurance field from the age of nineteen until the time of my enrollment at the seminary at age twenty-eight. I believe it was working in this field where I learned what I would describe as the power of listening. Listening to clients and their insurance needs helped me to assist many people throughout those years.

My desire to enlist in the military had never left me. So, shortly after I began working in insurance marketing, I chose the Marine Corps Reserve. While I had a relatively short enlistment, the training, especially the discipline, the sense of duty and service, and tenacity placed an indelible imprint deep within me. It remains to this day. It seemed that the inclination to serve further grew during my time in the Marine Corps. While I still possessed the inclination to serve as a priest, the call had not yet come. At the age of twenty-seven, almost immediately after getting married, and beginning a new chapter of life, including a new position as a commercial insurance representative, I received the call of our Lord Jesus Christ.

It came during the Lenten season of 1990. At first, I could not make sense of it. I was shocked and resisted it. I spoke with my parents, who advised me to remain focused on my career and marriage. It was my wife who could see that I was struggling. When she asked if there was something wrong, I told her that I thought our Lord was calling me to become a priest. I decided to make an appointment with my parish priest. He reminded me that God's call comes differently to each person. His call did not always align with the time we thought best. He provided me with examples of the call of the Holy Apostles of Jesus, who were invited to immediately leave behind what they were doing and follow Him. We had several appointments, and I was truly grateful for them.

After Pascha, it seemed that the call was intensifying. There seemed to be an urgency on God's part. It became clear that I needed to answer the call to follow Him. My wife agreed. In early June of 1990, I applied to the seminary, and two months later, on a humid New England morning, I took my first steps onto the campus. It was these thoughts that raced through my mind as Fr. Harakas spoke. I was convinced that I had both the inclination and the call to serve as a priest of our Lord. On the brief journey I had taken through my mind, by the time I had returned to attention, our orientation session was finished, and we were headed for lunch.

As I began my studies, I quickly began to feel as though I was at home on the seminary campus. The inspirational services and homilies in the chapel, the example set by the clergy of the school, and the knowledge being imparted to me about our Orthodox Christian faith further fueled my desire to serve as an Orthodox Christian priest. I would spend five years at Hellenic College-Holy Cross, finishing my undergraduate and graduate degrees. While they were not without difficulty and trials, I give thanks to God for those precious years. The inclination and the call were being confirmed beyond my person, in the priests who were teaching me and my brother seminarians.

As I approached graduation, a sense of fear came over me, and I began to ask the same questions that I had when I entered our seminary. "Did I truly have the call to become a priest?" "Would I be able to fulfill the myriad of duties that accompanied the priestly vocation?" "Can I truly fulfill this gargantuan responsibility that our Lord was placing on my weak shoulders?" After speaking with my spiritual father-confessor and some of my professors, including Fr. Harakas, and after much prayer, I petitioned for holy orders and was ordained to both the holy diaconate and as a presbyter in the fall of 1995, several months after seminary graduation.

As I began the priestly ministry as an assistant to Fr. George Nicozisin of blessed memory, the inclination and the call incarnated. Father George further guided and taught me with great patience and love during the infancy of my priesthood. He confirmed the inclination and the call. He saw something in me that I could not see.

I have had the unique privilege to serve our Lord's Church as His priest for twenty-nine years. It is the honor of honors, an honor of which I know I will never be truly worthy. Yet, the Lord continues to confirm the call He gave me thirty-four years ago. He continues to hold His holy hand towards me. He continues to invite: "Follow Me." If you have the inclination and the call, follow it, for it will enrich your life in ways beyond all imagination!

Father Michael Condos serves at
Three Hierarchs Church in Champaign, Illinois.

Father Michael Constantinides

My story begins in eighth grade. I was in Sunday school, and we were talking about the crucifixion. I asked my teacher, "If Christ said, 'Father, forgive them, for they know not what they are doing,' did that apply to Judas?" My Sunday school teacher, though very pious, could not answer the question and naturally referred me to my priest, Fr. Socrates Tsamutalis. He recommended that I come and be an altar boy.

In my home parish, Sunday school began following the Gospel reading, we had 900 families and they needed to remove the children to have room for the adults, so if you were in Sunday school you could not be in the altar and vice-versa. All this took place around Easter in 1983. While I was in the altar, Fr. Socrates continued my religious education and much to my dismay he made me do book reports. He would make me read the books published by the Department of Religious Education of the Archdiocese. These were thin books with titles like Doctrine or The Creed.

I served with Fr. Socrates throughout my high school career, and for sure he took me under his wing. He had me help with the sacraments, read psalms in orthros and many other things. One Sunday, as we were kneeling at the Divine Liturgy, I looked up as he was reading the prayers, and immediately I knew that I wanted to be a priest like him.

In 1988, as a high school senior, I applied to Hellenic College. It was the only school I applied to. Father continued to guide me and advise me throughout the process. Then, on Holy Friday of that year, between the Apokathelosis and the Lamentations service, the Lord called him from the earthly altar to the heavenly one. I was devastated, as I lost both my mentor and spiritual father! At his funeral on Bright Tuesday, the Dean of Hellenic College and Holy Cross, who was a classmate of Fr. Socrates, saw me in the altar and told me that he read my file on the plane ride over and I would be getting a letter of acceptance.

I know that many of my brothers have had experiences of a more tangible calling, but I was called through the love and nurturing of my priest. While I never found out the answer to my question until I entered seminary, I will always remember what Fr. Socrates taught me, and I will remember him in my prayers.

Father Michael Constantinides serves at Saint George Church in Rock Island, Illinois.

Father Panteleimon Dalianis

Also I heard the voice of the Lord, saying: "Whom shall I send, And who will go for Us?" Then I said, "Here am I! Send me" (Isaiah 6:8).

Just before the actual priest ordination service in the Divine Liturgy, the ordainee offers a message to the ordaining hierarch, sharing his thoughts, hopes, and gratitude for the great grace of ordination which he is about to receive. The words quoted above, from the Prophet Isaiah, formed the center of my own words on the day of my ordination.

My own path to ordination had many twists and turns, and it was only near the end of my pre-ordination life that it felt clear that ordination was the right path for me.

I grew up in a Greek Orthodox home. Both of my parents were cradle Orthodox, and we grew up going to Divine Liturgy most every Sunday. I served as an acolyte, attended Sunday school, and attended Fanari Camp. The parish where I grew up was a larger parish, and we always had two clergy. For most of my life, Fr. Emmanuel Lionakis was the senior priest, and there were a series of younger priests who were mentored under Fr. Emmanuel, who would then move on to their own parishes.

Likely the earliest influence I had in the direction of ordination was my interaction with these younger priests—Fr. Dean Hountalis and Fr. Alexios Gushes being the ones I remember best. These were the clergy with whom we did GOYA and altar boy training. As I was involved in the Boy Scouts as a youth, Fr. Dean Hountalis and I also worked together for me to complete the Alpha Omega Scouting award, which gave me even more opportunity to get to know our clergy.

I did not attend Hellenic College. Even though ordination had been a thought for me in middle school and early high school, by the end of my high school years other interests had clouded out thoughts of ordination. I attended Purdue University, graduating in 1993 with a bachelor's degree in economics. After my undergraduate studies, I returned home, not sure what direction I wanted to take in life. This part of my life turned out to be the most formative, in terms of my relationship to the Church and Christ.

A number of things happened on my path to ordination: I met a priest who would ultimately become my spiritual father and (eventually) sign my symartiria (this is the document a spiritual father signs for a spiritual child who is to be ordained, affirming the spiritual father's support for the ordinand). I also was recruited to teach high school Sunday school at St. Nectarios Church in Palatine, Illinois.

My spiritual Father, Fr. Theodore Petrides, introduced me to the Orthodox spiritual life. He guided me in reading the scriptures and other Orthodox books, he gave me a prayer rule and heard my confessions, and really became a second father to me.

Teaching Sunday school introduced me to ministry in a way that I had not been exposed to before. While I will admit to having zero background in teaching, the first year of teaching was very difficult (I didn't know what I was doing and always felt ill-prepared in class); but as time went on, and I developed relationships with the kids, I really fell in love with the ministry, and Sunday school class became one of the highlights of my week.

All of this culminated in what I would call my definitive calling, which happened in February of 1998, while I was attending the Chicago Metropolis Young Adult Conference. I remember being in one of the small-group discussions, and, all of a sudden, feeling a strong and clear sense that I needed to leave my secular job (at that time I was working for a small public relations firm in the Chicago suburbs) and go to seminary.

That summer (August 1998), I did just that. From the fall of 1998 through May of 2002, I attended Holy Cross Greek Orthodox School of Theology, receiving my Master of Divinity degree. My years at Holy Cross were important transition years for me, marking a decision in my life to no longer pursue a secular career, but rather a life of service through the Church. The liturgical life (especially my first year when we were in charge of the chapel for Holy Week) played a big role in my own growth as an Orthodox Christian. Many of my classmates and schoolmates have become close friends and koumbaroi.

After seminary, I spent one year in Greece studying the Greek language, and, in the middle of that year, I returned home to get married to my (now) Presvytera Konstantina.

I did not get ordained right out of seminary. It wasn't until four years after seminary that my wife and I felt ordination was the direction in which we were being called. Since then, we have served in four parishes and are thankful for the unique role we have been given to play in the lives of our flock.

Father Panteleimon Dalianis serves at Saints Constantine and Helen Church in Wauwatosa, Wisconsin.

S ince I was a young child, I looked forward to the day I would serve the body of Christ, the church, and the people of God. Many different priests served at Saint Nicholas Church in Oak Lawn, Illinois, my home parish. They set an example of what a priest should be. Ever since I can remember, I was always in church, whether it was a Sunday morning or a weekday liturgy on a major feast day, taking my yiayia to church. My reward was sitting next to her and listening to the entire service in Greek. My home parish was walking distance from where we lived. We could never use an excuse that we could not go to church for the Divine Liturgy, because when you live that close, there are no excuses, no matter how great they might seem—you were putting on your Sunday best to enter the Lord's home.

When I was in junior high, I felt a calling, a burning desire that I wanted something more than just going to church. I felt the need to be a servant to the people. It was a feeling that is so indescribable, but it was a feeling of being overjoyed, a feeling that I cannot express in words.

However, I had another feeling that was burning deep inside me, and that was to play sports. I struggled at times over this feeling, because many of the sports programs were held on Sundays back in the day. So for the next few years, I managed to play baseball and go to church.

Everything changed for me once I graduated and entered high school.

In high school, I was very active in sports. My freshman year in high school I was already playing on the varsity football team and wrestling on the junior varsity team, along with playing baseball and basketball. I also was fortunate enough to play for the village of Oak Lawn's baseball travel team. When I wasn't playing ball in high school, I was playing basketball for our Greek Orthodox church league. As I continued to play sports my freshman and sophomore years, I would always seek spiritual guidance from Father Dennis Strouzas, who was the parish priest at St. Nicholas church at that time. I also received guidance from Father Michael from the high school that I attended.

Mind you, I was the first born of four brothers, and thus whenever I wanted to play sports and not attend church, it was met with great resistance from both my parents. Not only did I take my yiayia to church whenever possible, but I also had to take my Italian grandmother (my nona) to Catholic mass on Saturdays. I was going to two different church services and enrolled in a Catholic high school where it was mandatory for students to go to mass. On the weekends, I drove both grandmothers to their churches. Sunday mornings, I would show up near the end of the Divine Liturgy for my priest to see me. This way I was in church, and then I could play in our basketball league. Not only that, but a new sports competition was instituted in the diocese and that was the Junior Olympics. It is held at our sister parish of Saint Constantine and Helen, and I played volleyball and shot put for St. Nicholas. We won the gold medal in both, but I remember vividly that I threw it one time and won the gold medal.

Time and time again, I was asked by Father Dennis Strouzas, "Where do you go on Sunday mornings when you are not in church?" My three younger brothers participated more in the religious aspect of the church than I did. They were altar boys on Sundays. I can honestly say I was never an altar boy.

In high school, I excelled in my studies, but more importantly I excelled in the sports that I played. I played football, and my positions were outside linebacker and fullback. I also wrestled all four years starting on the sophomore squad, but quickly moved up to junior varsity and varsity squads.

In 1983, we were state champions, and again in 1984. Academically I was one of the top ten percent in my class, graduating twentieth out of 585 students and scoring a 30 on my ACT exam. I was offered numerous scholarships across the country. Now I thought I had my whole future planned out for me right before my eyes. It is painful to say, but church had just become an afterthought. As I entered my senior year, I knew what I wanted to do with my life. I wanted to attend a top school and play football or baseball and get a law degree. I began to have this inner struggle within myself. Once again, I felt a strong urge to return to church, there was a force pushing me toward the Church in every direction and being out of the Church for so long, I was too embarrassed to show my face. Whatever this feeling was, I was going through it and kept to myself. Football season was starting, and my focus was on that.

No sooner did the season start than I was injured. I remember that day as if it were yesterday. The medics came out to the field and put a neck brace on my neck. I knew that I was not going to be playing football again. The CT scans confirmed my thoughts; they showed my lower back had four bulging discs and injuries to my neck and shoulder.

When I was brought to Christ Hospital, my parish priest, Father Dennis, was just being transferred to New York, and our parish was waiting for the new priest, who was Fr. Gabriel Karambis. The next Saturday morning at 6:00 am, I heard this deep voice saying to the nurse, "Is he sleeping?" I opened my eyes, and there was Fr. Byron from Saints Constantine and Helen at my bedside. I explained to him what happened, and the wisdom and guidance he gave me helped me make my decision.

Suddenly, it felt like a huge weight was lifted from me. It was now my senior year in high school, and knowing football was no longer an option for me, I wrestled and played basketball and baseball. At one point, I went and talked with the priest at my high school; his name was Fr. Michael. He invited me on a retreat at Beret College. He explained that here we would be in solitude and have the opportunity, without distractions, to be able to pray and seek guidance from fellow priests who were attending. Unbeknownst to me, Fr. Michael had contacted all the parents and asked them to write us letters. The letter was to say how they viewed their son and what their hopes and aspirations were for him. My letter from my mother was a little bit different; it seemed as if she were offering a confession to me. Please, do not get me wrong, I love my mother and father, but they have a funny way of showing love back. I do not know if it is from their own personal upbringing by their parents, but I do remember my mother telling me that even though my father never showed his emotions toward me by saying, "I love you, I'm proud of you," or sat down to see how I was doing in school or if anything was bothering me, he did love me. It was kind of funny and even whimsical that my mother wrote on his behalf.

My father showed me around the restaurant from the ground up. I bussed tables, mopped floors—you name it, I did it. Finally, he trusted me to start cooking, and for that I am grateful, because I developed a great love for working in the kitchen. During this time, there were many opportunities to tell him that I had decided I want something else for myself; so while I was at Barrett College on this retreat, I opened the letter my mother wrote and began to read it, not knowing how they really felt about me. It is hard now to discuss or even think about the words. They were all on this paper that my mother wrote on their behalf. As I said, I had never heard the words "I am proud of you," or, "Good job," but I realized where their hearts were, and I understood them for the very first time.

While on this retreat, I also realized that the scholarships to the schools I wanted to go were no longer offered to me. I did get offered academic scholarships, but I soon learned that as the first-born to parents that came to this country from Greece and Italy, going away to school was not an option. I searched my heart to see what direction my life would take me. For two years, even while in high school, I worked at my father's restaurant in downtown Chicago as a cook during the summer months and on weekends. Then I got a job as a cook at an Italian restaurant near my home. Frank and Joe, who are the owners of this restaurant, sent me to culinary school to receive my culinary degree. So I began taking classes at a culinary school in Chicago after my graduation. It was to be a two-year course, but I finished it in a year-and-a-half. My goal was to go away to college, work on my undergraduate degree, and then work on my law degree. Something was missing though. I had an empty feeling within me, and at first, I thought it was not playing sports. That was not the case; I felt something pulling me to the church, and one day as I sat in the pew, I heard the words of Christ saying "many are called but few are chosen." For some odd reason that saying stuck in my mind for weeks. I finally sat down with Fr. Gabriel Karambis, my parish priest, and explained to him what I was thinking of doing. Fr. Gabriel had other thoughts on his mind. He immediately purchased a round trip ticket from Chicago to Boston for me to visit the Hellenic College Holy Cross.

Upon visiting the seminary, I felt that this was to be my new home. The only thing that was on my mind on the way home was how to tell my parents. My grandmother Sturino, my Italian grandmother, always told me that she saw me as a priest, ever since I was a little boy, and that one day that is what I would become.

After many years of struggling with this decision, including years of prayer and seeking guidance from my spiritual elders, I finally realized that I was being called to serve God. I realized what an awesome experience this would be. I can remember the words of Isaiah that stood out in my mind.: I will greatly rejoice in the Lord ;my soul shall be joyful in my God. (Isaiah 61:10) I remember also reading from Proverbs, "unto you man I call; my voice is to the sons of man. All you simple, understand wisdom; and you fools be understanding heart. Listen and I will speak of excellent things (Proverbs 8:4-6).

I remember the day when my application came to the house to be filled out and being told that I would have to make an appointment to see his Grace Bishop Iakovos of Chicago of blessed memory in order to get his recommendation. I knew His Grace from his many visits to our parish, but I never spoke to him about my feelings about the priesthood. He too gave me some sound advice to follow my heart.

Thus I decided to make every effort to search my heart and listen to the call from God. With my heart open and deep searching, I found myself. There was no more struggle about what I wanted to do with my life. I have found myself walking along a certain path, and that path has brought me to our Lord. I knew the path that I had chosen was not going to be an easy one but rather it would be one where I might stumble and fall at times and may even question myself. In order to follow our Lord, I understood the great burden that I was taking upon myself, as I moved forward in His footsteps. I understood that no man is worthy of these mysteries and responsibilities, but I also took to heart Christ's saying in Matthew (10:38-38) "Anyone who does not take his cross and follow me is not worthy of me. Whoever finds his life and loses it, and whoever loses his life for my sake will find it." I have not come to this point in my life on my own nor do I take these words of Christ lightly. These were words that rang out in my ears when I sat down and when Fr. Byron visited me in the hospital.

I thought I had many friends. When I decided what path my life was now heading for, my great group of friends was no longer there; but I can say this, I did have my core group of friends from my parish of Saint Nicholas. The friends I grew up with since I was a young child respected my decision. I told my friends of my decision to pursue this calling to the priesthood.. Again I was reminded that many are called, but few are chosen, and I was wondering if I was going to be one of the few that would be chosen by God to serve His church.

I found it easy to tell friends and even some members of my family, but as for my immediate family, my brothers and my mother and father, I was very hesitant. I do not know if it was fear or disappointment I felt when I had to tell my parents that I made the decision to enter the seminary. I knew this road was going to be difficult, but I did not know how difficult it was going to become when it came to my family and friends. It's funny—when times are good people are always around you, but when times are bad then you know who your real friends are, and, boy, did I learn who my friends were and those who stuck by me. I do not know too much of what happened to the others; I pray for them.

Deep down I realized I did have a support group around me. I had very close bond with clergy such as Fr. Isaiah Chronopoulos, Fr. Gabriel Karambis, Fr. Byron Papanikolaou, Fr. Nick Jonas, Fr. Nick Lilias, Fr. Alexios Gushes, and Fr. George.

There were just three people that I needed to sit down and talk to: my parents and my girlfriend at the time. I still didn't know how to face my father. I sat down with my mother and explained to her my feelings and the path I had chosen to take. Of course, she was in shock, yet she was very supportive and loving toward my decision. It was now time to tell my father. and I kept putting it off over several weeks; then it became months, but the time was approaching, and I would have to pack up and move to Brookline, Massachusetts. I went to my girlfriend's house to tell her my decision and what my intentions would be for the future. She was not completely supportive, but said it is your life and you should try and see if this is what you want.

Now the weeks and days were approaching for me to get ready to leave for Boston. I told the owners that I worked for at the Italian restaurant, and they were kind enough to set me up with a job in the Italian section of Boston know as the North End at a restaurant called La Piccola Venezia. Now my departure for school was even closer than I thought. Instead of leaving at the end of August, I was now leaving In June in order to go to Boston and start work at the Italian restaurant.

As I was preparing to leave, I began to struggle with this decision once again. I was asking myself if I was doing the right thing. I remember working for my father at the restaurant and getting up early in the morning. I would leave the house in Oak Lawn and head down to the city where our restaurant was at 4:30 am; there you would see many homeless people sleeping along the streets. When I saw this, I remembered the gospel lesson, "When I was hungry you fed me, when I was thirsty you gave me drink, and when I was sick you visited me . . ." So, at 4:45 in the morning, I opened the front doors even though the restaurant didn't open till 5:30. I was there alone, so I took it upon myself to cook for about ten people. The next day those ten people grew to 30 people, and I needed to call for help serving them food. I had one of the waitresses come in early, swore her to secrecy and gave her an extra hundred-dollar tip to keep her mouth quiet, and we served these homeless people. Within two weeks, it grew to over 100 people in the restaurant. I was just days away from leaving for Boston, and I still hadn't told my father I was going to the seminary. When I saw all these happy faces eating a warm meal ordering whatever they wanted on the menu, it did not bother me. I felt it was the right thing to do because maybe one of these people was Christ himself who was sitting in the restaurant having breakfast. One day my father decided to come in a little bit earlier to work, and when he saw around 120 homeless people sitting in the booths eating, he just about lost his temper. Immediately he came into the kitchen and pulled me to the side and began to explain to me how much dinner or breakfast cost, and my response was, "What does it matter, you are not paying for it. I paid for it." He looked at me with bewilderment on his face and said, "What are you talking about?" I said, "Ask the waitress; she is getting paid $100 to be here to serve and is getting paid from my pocket. All the meals that were being served were from my pocket (of course I used the money I made from my other job at the Italian restaurant), and I made sure that none of the food they were eating was from his refrigerator. Rather, I paid for it from the purveyors. All he could keep thinking was now they are going to come every day. I responded, "No, this is their last week here, and they know it, because I will no longer be here. I will be moving." I have no idea what overcame me to say what I said, but I thought there was no time like the present to tell him what was going on with my life. I said, "Dad, we come from a lineage of clergy in our family. Your great-grandfather was a priest, and your uncle was a priest. In fact, there were several family members who were priests, and if you ask my Uncle Nick, he claims that one of the bishops of Greece was our relative." I do not know how true that was, but nonetheless I continued my confession to him by saying, "Dad, this is my calling right now to serve God." The look on his face was not one of happiness or curiosity, but one of shock and a little anger. He turned and said, "Why don't you just leave and go home," so I left and went home. This was Friday morning, and I was leaving on Monday. Those were the last words he spoke to me for over three years. For whatever reason, he did not want me to go into the priesthood; he always saw me going in to law school or working in some restaurant, but never as a priest. Monday morning came, and my mother was up early to say goodbye to me. My father would not come out of the room until I was gone. I can still remember the look on his face and how disappointed he was with me.

After arriving in Boston, I called my mother and my girlfriend to let them know I arrived in one piece. After a few weeks, I drove home for Columbus Day weekend to surprise everyone. Of course, I had no interaction with my father, so I figured I would just go out with my girlfriend. We talked about what the role of a priest was and the role of a presvytera. It was during this conversation that her true feelings came out. She did not know if she could go on with this relationship knowing that she had doubts. Upon hearing this, we got back in the car, and I drove her home. I walked her to the front door, and I told her that because of her doubts, I could not see her anymore. If would not be fair to stay in a relationship knowing what my intentions are, and it would not be fair to me knowing that she would not be able to follow me in serving Christ. I said it was best that we just say goodbye

after being in a relationship for six years. As hard as it was, the reality was that this calling for me might not have been for her. I returned to Boston to continue my studies, and by the grace of God, after a few years, I met my soulmate, my best friend and presvytera. She married me knowing the struggle before us, and her devotion to the church and her faith is a comfort to me and goes beyond words; because of this, I chose this woman to be my wife. She has completely changed me today for the better. I am not always very good with words to express my love for her, but without her strength and love I do not think I could not have continued this journey alone. She stood by my side during my years of study.

I would be remiss if I did not mention my father once again. As I said earlier, I left for the seminary, and my father did not speak to me for three years, but something had changed within him. My father became a source of love and strength for me, and even though he did not speak to me for years, he ended up supporting my decision to become a Greek Orthodox priest. Since then he has been there to help me in every hour of need. There was one point when I questioned myself again, if I was making the right decision. I wondered if I should just pack up and come home and go back and enter law school. In the end, it was my father who encouraged me to stay strong and accept this great gift which God has given to me.

As I wrote this, it brought back so many memories of good and difficult decisions I had to make. My journey in life began with sports, and that was leading me down a certain path until I was plagued with injuries, but the burning call within me lead me down a whole new path. This path that Christ showed me through many signs, led me to the holy priesthood. These have been the most rewarding moments of my life, and I am most grateful to God that he found me worthy enough to serve at His Holy Altar.

Father Sotirios Dimitriou serves at
Assumption Church in Homer Glen, Illinois.

Father Pavlos Borislav Dinkov

When I was a child, we did not attend church much. All we did was go to light a candle at times with my parents and then stop by to have lunch. Nevertheless, it was the occasional pilgrimage trips my grandmother would take me on with her, around the country, where I first began to sense the mystery of the "Divine". At other times, I would notice my grandmother doing a strict fast (no food, or little bread), but I wouldn't make sense of what she was doing until much later in my life. I also remember going to Pascha services in the village of my grandparents. There were many people gathered back at that time, but I would not know why we were all there. Again, this would make sense to me many years later, when I would embark on a search of my own for the God who loves me. This is how it is with us people. We have many experiences as children that we call upon later in life to form us into who we become. In my case, if things had continued on the trajectory I described, I don't think I would have been called to a life of a Christian or to the Priesthood. This is where the good Lord acted to wake me up because He had planned something else for me.

When I was about twelve, my parents divorced, and my mother left. She went to seek happiness elsewhere. This was a time when I felt profound sorrow, yet for the first time I began to learn what hope is. A friend of my father's, whom I would call my Aunt Theodora, became my guide and support. She was an old woman with a family who lived a simple life yet had a gift to help and heal those in need. Her words to me in the years to come would be like the words of the Lord. She encouraged me and believed in me at times when I had no one else to believe in me. She would tell me about God and how He worked in her own life. She would direct me to go and ask for prayers and services for the priests to read for me for well-being and prosperity; she would instruct me to get holy water from the church, and to go to services. Despite this all, what will be the greatest gift to me, of that time of my life, was that she was able to instill in me the love that God had for me. It was and still is the Lord himself who spoke through her. This gave me confidence to overcome the hardships that were around me daily. I could never repay her that goodness or repay the Lord for His mercy.

In this way a desire awoke in me to serve the Lord that Aunt Theodora served—the same one who gave me hope and love when I had nothing. Yet this desire would take twenty years to grow and manifest fully when our beloved Metropolitan Nathanael laid his hands on me, or rather the hands of the Lord, to ordain me first a deacon on July 26, 2020, at the feast of the Dormition of Saint Anna and the memory of deaconess Olympia, and then a priest on October 4, 2020, when we honor the great martyr Hierotheos of Athens and venerable Paul the Simple, among others.

The journey that led me to this greatest of honors bestowed on men, namely, to be in service of the Lord, was not short; only through persistence and God's grace have I seen the fruits of my still imperfect love for Jesus.

At this point I'd like to continue the story from where I left off. The period of my life between twelve and eighteen was not easy either. You may not believe when I say this, but my family became a subject of directed demonic attacks through incantations that have left a deep imprint on me. I could compare it to watching Harry Potter in real life. The things I saw and experienced during that time could have been a dead end for me, if it weren't for the persistent love and guidance of my aunt. In those years I developed an even deeper sense of the mystical and divine world we live in and love for the One who has set it all in motion, but most of all a profound desire to find all I could about Him.

When I was nineteen, the Lord directed me to come to the United States to study. I borrowed money to buy my plane ticket. I worked through the summers, sometimes more than a hundered hours a week, and paid my undergraduate tuition, all with the help of the Lord. I felt Him helping me, yet I was still afraid to follow him fully. That fear also made me choose my area of studies to be computer science rather than psychology, for example. I tried to make sure I would find work after graduation, and I did. Yet, my heart was elsewhere. I longed for the seminary; I longed to get closer to God and to know Him better.

One winter morning as I was driving on I-787, and passing over a bridge, I hit black ice, and my car began spinning out of control. Fortunately, there were no cars around me and the cars which were behind were able to stop. My car also stopped, but it was facing the traffic. There was a moment when I had lost control of the car and was wondering if I would end up flying from the bridge or if a car would come smashing at me from the side. In this tense moment, I felt my life flash by in an instant, and there was a cry from my soul to God that said to Him that I had not done anything good yet and that I had not served Him yet. I pleaded with Him in that single moment to let me continue, and He did. I was able to start the car, turn around and get out of harm's way.

This is probably the foundational moment of my resolve to leave the earthly studies and direct my gaze to the divinely inspired ones. I learned how short life is and how little time we have been given to do something good.

The last example that I will use to illustrate the hand of the Almighty One was when I challenged Him. It was when I found out that I would need to pay $120,000 for my education. It cost $30,000 a year and I could not take student loans. I remember when I vividly lifted my eyes to Him and said "Lord, I cannot afford this, obviously I can't go to the seminary then." Two weeks later, the Lord introduced me to Mr. Christopher Kendris, who would become family to me and I to him. He is the author of the 501 Spanish and French Verbs series—a very educated man and a scholar. He took me under his wing and guess what – he paid for my schooling. I will be forever grateful to him for his love and support. Would you believe if I told you that he passed away within a week of my graduation from the seminary? This is a person who lived by the words "It is more blessed to give, than to receive." I call him my Greek grandfather.

To sum it up, I would say that it is hard to answer the call from above. It took me many years to do so. I wish I had done it sooner. I had lost much time in being afraid. It is hard to not fear, but let us always remember that the Lord sustains us all. He is always reaching out to us and in all circumstances He has His hand extended. All we need to do is extend our hand back to Him. We just need to learn to trust Him. So many times in the Gospels he says, "Do not fear." All one needs to do is believe Him. After all, I firmly believe that the only one who can satisfy the human heart is the One who made it. May whoever it is that is reading this story, may you be blessed with courage and boldness to follow your path with the Lord.

Father Pavlos Dinkov serves at Holy Trinity Church in Fond du Lac, Wisconsin and Saint Spyridon Church in Sheboygan, Wisconsin.

Father George Dokos

A s an Orthodox priest, I am often asked by both Orthodox and non-Orthodox why I became a priest. The question has taken many forms: "So, what made you decide to become a priest?" "Why are you a priest?" "Was your dad a priest?" and other like questions. Depending on to whom I am speaking, and the amount of time available, my answer has varied a bit, but it has always remained consistent. Now, for the first time, I am putting it down on paper.

I don't consider my call to serve the Church anything particularly exciting, or perhaps even vastly different from the stories of other priests' callings. Nevertheless, it is mine, so unique, just as everyone's story is unique. Where to begin? I think we'll start with my very first memory of what can only be called an existential experience of awe.

The exact year escapes me, and therefore, I can only speculate as to my precise age, but I venture to say I was around ten years old. It was a Sunday morning, and I was serving in the altar during the Divine Liturgy. For some reason I happened to look directly at the celebrating priest–I was off to his left–in a way that I had never looked at him (or seen him?) before. Perhaps it was during the Great Litany as he was offering up petitions on behalf of all the faithful, perhaps it was during the Trisagion Hymn, or perhaps it was during the prayer of the Cherubic Hymn (I will never be sure), but what I saw, what I fixedly gazed upon, was a man caught up in ecstatic prayer. His robes gleamed, his face shone with solemnity, love, and joy, his head was intently upraised toward the eastward heavens, and I was caught up with him in his prayer. It's as if I was pulled into his very experience of God and God's divine grace. I can see it, feel it, even now, and to meditate upon that experience moves me to tears.

I will never be able to do justice to that moment–that ineffable moment which seems to have frozen me in time–through words, because, as I said, it is a deeply personal and existential experience that will forever only be my own. I can certainly say that, from that moment on, I knew in my deepest self that that was what I wanted, needed, to do: to stand before the holy altar table, before the very throne of God, in worship and in intercession.

Rewinding a bit, I cannot fail to acknowledge and thank my parents for giving me the greatest gift in the universe: the gift of Christianity. I will never know what it means to live outside of grace and outside of God's kingdom, because I was baptized as an infant and joined to Christ at that earliest age. This cannot be overlooked or minimized in its significance. However, my parents not only had me baptized, but raised me in the life of the Church. Without fail we were at Divine Liturgy on Sunday mornings ten minutes before it began and always on time to at least hear the Great Doxology sung by the choir (my father, although born in Greece, was not your typical Greek; he was punctual! And therefore, so am I).

Being raised in the Orthodox Christian faith clearly impacted me, but so did serving in the altar (as evidenced from the story above). What I haven't mentioned yet is the fact that my parish priest would pick me up early on Sunday mornings on his way to church so that I could arrive with him and prepare the church. I would light the oil lamps and candles, prepare the censer, even read some of the prayers of the Proskomide with him as he prepared the Holy Gifts. Somehow, I, too, was being prepared for a life in the priestly ministry of the Church.

Then came a point in my life that I decisively felt that pursuing the priesthood was the path for me (in fact, over time, this calling intensified to such a degree that I felt almost as though I had no choice; I knew that nothing else would ever fulfill me; there was even an unseen compulsion, the "Woe to me if I do not preach the Gospel" of St. Paul). While in my high school years I met with my priest and expressed to him this exact sentiment. "I want to be a priest," I said. Elated and with a contented smile on his face, he paused, and then he spoke to me about the parable of the Good Samaritan. "The man beaten and bleeding by the side of the road is the Church, and she needs to be ministered unto."

I will never forget how he spoke to me about the Church, how she needs spiritual leaders and servants, ministers, to take care of her, and the Church is the body of Christ, the body of believers that I have been called to serve.

Father George Dokos serves at
Holy Apostles Church in Westchester, Illinois.

Father David Eynon

My call to the priesthood begins with a carnation. On Holy Friday night, as the parish was cleaning and getting things ready for Holy Saturday morning, Fr. George Pyle asked me to tear apart a pile of leftover carnations from the *kavouklion*. This being my first Holy Week, he explained that this seemingly destructive task was a good — they were to be added to a basket full of bay leaves that the priest would use the next day. I was the only person on flower duty, and I made sure that every left over carnation was collected, torn apart, and placed in the basket.

The next morning, when I heard "Arise, O Lord, and inherit the earth!" a shower of leaves and petals flew over the iconostasis in my direction. I was shocked to see a whole carnation in their midst. I was even more flustered when it hit me in nose. It was at this moment that I knew God wanted me to not only embrace Christianity, but to become Orthodox.

While my mother was Presbyterian and my dad understood the necessity of God in order to explain his understanding of the world,

I was not raised in a Christian home. I did not go to church outside of Christmas and by the time I was a teenager, I had rejected the Christianity with which I was familiar. Despite the fact that I argued against Christ with conviction, I was actually unsatisfied with the answers the secular world had to offer about life, the universe, and everything. Like St. Justin the Philosopher, I went looking into every type of explanation of reality I could get my hands on. There were moments when I thought I was satisfied, but once I started pushing, every world-view would come crashing down. That is, until I encountered St. Irenaeus of Lyon. When I read his apologetics against the Gnostics, I distinctly remember saying to myself, "Crap. I need to take Christianity seriously now." So I began to look for the church St. Irenaeus was talking about. It wasn't until I found Orthodox Christianity that I found this church. Orthodoxy wasn't afraid of my questions. I might not have liked some of the answers, but there was always an answer. The more I pushed, the more it pushed back. Like St. Justin the Philosopher, I finally found the philosophy that would explain everything. As I continue to ask questions to this day, Orthodoxy continues to provide answers, and I more profoundly appreciate why St. Justin was so at home in the Orthodox Church. Finally, as that carnation hit my nose, I found myself saying, "Okay, God, I give."

In short order, I was baptized, met my wife at Church, and got married. I served in the altar and was eventually elected to the parish council. In the meantime, people started to ask if I were going to become a priest. I always demurred, because such a life was never something I would have considered possible, especially from someone who had spent the majority of his life denying Christ. I soon found out that the question wasn't being asked by these people, but rather the Holy Spirit Himself. Over one summer, God sent several priests from several jurisdictions to serve at our parish for a variety of reasons. *All* of them asked me when I was going to be a priest. The most direct looked me in the eye and indignantly said, "When are you going to stop being a priest in a business suit?" I would later tell him his influence on my decision to become a priest, and he didn't remember ever saying that to me.

The final straw was when I baptized my first child. I was holding her in the narthex during "The Making of a Catechumen," because she was being fussy and was only calm while I held her. A little boy, who had only ever known me as an acolyte serving in the altar, tugged at his father's sleeve and asked, "Why isn't the priest wearing his robe?" Again, I found myself saying, "Okay, God, I give." I started the process to apply to Holy Cross Greek Orthodox School of Theology.

This application process requires several things, of which there are a number that are completely out of the applicant's control. Our lease for our current apartment was coming to an end, we didn't have a place to live in Boston, my wife had yet to find a job in Boston, and we didn't have the money to pay for tuition. The world kept pressuring us to move on from the decision to go to Holy Cross, and we kept trying to control things we couldn't. After a particularly stressful day, I gave up. I said once again, "Okay, God, I give. If this is going to happen, you are going to have to take care of it." The very next day, I received my acceptance letter, an apartment on campus, and a financial package that allowed us to afford going. Once we stepped on campus, my wife, newly graduated with a Masters in Library Science, was immediately offered a job at the Archbishop Iakovos Library as a Librarian. Not only had God provided a job, but one that my wife could walk to.

Everything that I have, everything that I am today, is dependent upon God. This is the lesson God wanted me to learn, that He continues to teach me. Through seminary, I did not succeed merely on my own skill. Only by trusting in God did I make any strides. My ordinations were the same. Both happened on His schedule, not mine (I was told on a Thursday I would be ordained a deacon on that next Sunday). To this day, I still find myself saying, "Okay, God, I give."

So, every Holy Saturday morning, as I throw carnation petals and bay leaves high into the air, I cry out in joy, "Arise, O Lord, and inherit the earth!" because God chose me, a sinner who once denied him, to be his priest.

Father David Eynon serves at
Annunciation Church in Decatur, Illinois.

Father Panayiotis Hasiakos

As a child, my family went to church on Sundays. Looking back, I continue to be amazed at the impact this weekly routine had on my life. We often think of going to church as merely an external action, but through experience, I have seen that this external action (of bringing ourselves physically into the Divine Liturgy) opens a door to spiritual transformation and God's involvement in our life.

Weekly church and Sunday school attendance was essentially my only church involvement as a child. I did not participate in any other ministries or events, but attending church with my family and relatives remained a foundational part of my life.

When I was in high school, I participated in the St. John Chrysostom Oratorical Festival at our parish, which was the first time the church challenged me to apply my intellectual abilities to our faith in a rigorous way. The topic I wrote about was the role of the Theotokos in our salvation.

This undertaking was extremely meaningful and satisfying, and it had an unexpected benefit: it yielded me a prize of a free trip to our Archdiocese's Ionian Village summer camp, which took place during the summer between my senior year of high school and freshman year of college. This was a formative and life-changing experience in two ways. First, I experienced the joy of being with peers in a beautiful and ecclesiastical environment. Second, I felt the presence of God and His holiness as we made pilgrimages to visit important churches and monasteries, many times having the privilege to venerate holy relics and hear the words of priests and monks who showed us their love and hospitality. A simple comment from one of my counselors also had a tremendous impact on my college years, which were about to begin. He said that even college students need to go to church weekly. The simplicity and truth of this statement echoed within me, and I felt validated that it was not only "okay", but necessary for me to be resolute in attending church on campus and growing in my faith. As the camp session closed, I tasted the joy of Byzantine chanting, the love of which came back with me on my flight home, and I started learning music notation with our parish's chanter.

At college, my love for the faith grew deeper through sharing in worship and discussions with other Orthodox Christian students my age, especially through the campus ministry of the Orthodox Christian Fellowship. This was the first time I was surrounded by people my age who were thirsting for a deeper knowledge and experience of Orthodoxy, even in the midst of the many distractions and academic demands of campus life. Attending College Conference at the Antiochian Village retreat center was yet another profound and transformative experience. All of

this was fortified by the presence of a loving, intelligent, and dedicated young priest at my local parish.

From this point forward, things developed naturally; it was a continuation of the growth that had begun, with my faith being nurtured by both peers and clergy. As an undergraduate student, I was within a triangle of three things that I loved: physics, medicine, and theology. I pursued all three of them during my time on campus, leaving all three doors open (high school teaching, medical school, and seminary).

For me, discerning my path forward was always a combination of excitement and uncertainty. While many of my peers were able to articulate their plans for study and future work with simplicity and in a very matter-of-fact way, I was never able to do this. I felt something intense going on inside me, that God had placed a flame of interest inside me for all of the aforementioned areas, but somehow things were not clicking into place. The only thing to do was to embrace one step at a time, attend to everything with diligence and sincerity, and allow God to work through my mentors and the many other good people He had placed around me.

By the end of my undergraduate studies, at the time that I was in the midst of taking the practice MCAT in anticipation of applying for medical school, I reached the point of feeling at peace with my next step. I decided not to take the MCAT, but to embrace my love for physics and teaching and apply for a master's degree in secondary education. Though I had seriously considered going first for theological studies (to use as a foundation for helping as a lay person in the Church), I decided to simply stay on campus and complete a one-year master's and certification program to become a physics teacher. My plan still kept two of the doors open: I would work as a teacher and become involved at my parish as a chanter and lay person, remaining open to theological studies if God presented me the opportunity.

Arriving back in Chicago, I taught high school physics for four years at a public high school in the western suburbs. These were wonderful years in which I was able to do meaningful work and continue growing in my faith. The next major event in this phase was crossing paths with a long- time friend, now my wife, Presvytera Nikolia. In some ways, I felt that both of us were simply following God's path in our lives, and that He brought those paths together in the life of the Church. Presvytera was also a high school teacher at the time who shared the same love for the Church and for our faith. Once we became engaged, we realized that both of had a desire to go to Boston for further study, and so it seemed that God was presenting the opportunity for us to do what we had desired for some time. After our wedding in the summer of 2012, we moved to Boston for me to enroll in the Master of Divinity program at Holy Cross, and for her to enroll at Boston College for a master's in religious education.

This was still a continuation of the difficult process of discerning God's path forward. I enrolled at Holy Cross with the philosophy of taking one step at a time. What was clear was that I had a deep desire to study theology. I did not come to campus with a sense of certainty that the priesthood was God's will in my life. On the contrary, it was a time of prayer and contemplation of this serious question, filled with hesitations, all of which were echoed and validated in the required reading prior to enrolling: St. John Chrysostom's homilies on the priesthood.

As time passed during my studies, I felt extremely blessed by the campus life and my theological education. I often felt a kind of anxiety thinking about how I could possibly seize all of the knowledge and study I desired within three or four years. This insatiable thirst to study the faith and especially the Church Fathers led me to stay on campus for a second degree (ThM), all the while considering the possibility of doctoral work.

Things finally settled a little bit within me during my year on campus doing the ThM degree, and I felt that my theological education—though it is something that is never "complete"—had provided me with an excellent foundation, and I began feeling open to entering parish life, and despite my hesitations I also began to feel an openness to ordination.

At that point, I departed from the beloved seminary campus, continuing my thesis work remotely, and entered parish life, being ordained a deacon in February of 2017 and a priest in June of the same year.

That is the story, in rough outline, of the path that led me to ordination. It was not filled with obvious or thundering milestones of revelation but more with the quiet presence of God in my life, gently encouraging me forward one step at a time. From this point of view, I think what I experienced is common to the life of every Christian seeking God and striving to do His will. The priesthood is indeed a lofty calling, something of which none of us are worthy, but I believe there is, in a sense, no calling more lofty than the one God has given each of us. There is nothing more lofty than embracing the mystery of the present moment in our life, in which God is at work and trying to take us somewhere. He speaks to us in the voice of a quiet breeze (cf. 1 Kings 19:12) and shows us only a little bit at a time (cf. Gen. 12:1). These are the aspects that used to cause me the greatest anxiety, but now I also find them to be the most beautiful part of the life in

Christ. As difficult as it is to approach life in this way, I am grateful to God for everything. There is nothing more beautiful and grounding than to know that He is ours and we are His, and that each moment of our life is an extension of the prayer, "Thy will be done." Glory to Him for all things!

Father Panayiotis Hasiakos serves at
Assumption Church in East Moline, Illinois.

I was born to parents with quite different backgrounds. My father was a Protestant as a child, but essentially agnostic (and leaning toward atheism), when I was growing up. Thankfully, he became more open toward Christ in his later years. My mother was raised as a committed Greek Orthodox Christian. She had her children baptized into the Orthodox faith as babies and inspired us through her love for Christ and His Church. I remember rides home from services, in which she enthusiastically spoke to us about God's love for us and told us what a blessing it was that we were part of Christ's Church as Orthodox Christians. She said that God loved us more than we could imagine, and that we should love Him in return. She also said that we could enter any profession we wanted someday, but that Christ and His Church were precious treasures on which we should never turn our backs.

Meanwhile, my home church community of the Holy Trans-figuration in Mason City, IA, was blessed to have a kind and dedicated priest in the person of Fr. Gregory Champion, of blessed memory. I remember liking and respecting him. When I was seven years old,

I began thinking that I wanted to be a priest as well. Naturally, this initial impulse was immature, and my motivations were far from pure. Being a priest looked fun and not too demanding (little did I know!). The attention a priest receives in his capacity as a leader also appealed to me. My parents warned me, though, that serving as a priest involves a lot of work and dedication. They also said that not all of the attention a priest receives is positive. One time, I playfully told my father that I should sit at the head of the table during dinner, since I was going to be a priest. He told me that priests should be servants, so that I should sit last at the table. The words of my father stuck with me, and I still ponder them to this day.

Along with the more selfish motivations in my heart, though, something else was also there. I felt drawn to the beauty of the services, and I was attracted to the sense of depth that I perceived in our faith and practices. Moreover, the thought of dedicating my life to the God who created us and loves us seemed right to me. Little things I recall include loving Bible stories, feeling moved by the "Jesus of Nazareth" television series, serving as an altar boy, and wearing towels at my home to "vest as a priest."

After some time, my interest in the priesthood waned. I am not entirely sure why this happened. One component, however, was the initial excitement wearing off. Meanwhile, my parents divorced and remarried, my interests became more secular, and fitting in with peers became more important to me. I enjoyed the activities that many kids my age engaged in: playing games and various sports with other children in my neighborhood, going roller skating on weekends (it was the late seventies!), and watching movies, just to name a few.

In seventh grade, I participated in school sports, where it quickly became apparent that my abilities were limited. Frankly, I was miserable in school sports, but I kept at them, lacking the courage to quit, given that my peers seemed to enjoy them so much. Having slogged through a season of school football, wrestling, and the beginnings of track and field, I finally worked up the strength to stop, and I decided that my desire to fit in would no longer dictate how I lived my life. This was a time of liberation and self- reflection. It was also when I once again began to feel the drawing of my heart toward the priesthood. This coincided with the departure of Fr. Gregory Champion from our parish. As we said our goodbyes, he told me to invite him to my ordination. Father Gregory's surprising request led toward some serious contemplation.

In the ensuing months, I felt increasingly certain that I should become a priest. I saw Jesus as the most important person in my life, and I wanted to grow in my relationship with Him. I desired to offer my life to Him and immerse myself in Him; serving as a priest seemed like the most fitting way to do this. I loved spending time at the church, especially serving as an altar boy. Religious education classes were also deeply interesting to me, and I greatly enjoyed reading about Church teachings, history, the spiritual life, and our liturgical traditions. The priests who served our parish during my teen years were Fathers Constantine Palassis, James Tsoulos, and Emmanuel Lillios, who were very supportive and provided valuable guidance.

As one might imagine, my adolescence was characterized by a mixture of joyful times and periods of great struggle. My relationship with God often vacillated. I sometimes wondered if I had the qualities needed to serve as a priest, or if I even wanted to be a priest. For a while, I strongly considered the monastic life, going so far as to visit Mount Athos, which was a deeply rewarding experience. This visit took place right before I went to seminary. In time, though, it became clear that my calling was to serve the Lord as a priest. It was not simply a matter of what I wanted to do with my life. In fact, the thought of going in any other direction seemed as if I would be turning away from God and His will for me. Despite my unworthiness, despite my insufficiencies, I resolved to offer whatever I had to the service of the Lord, trusting in His mercy and putting my life in His hands.

Father Basil Hickman serves at
Saint George Church in Des Moines, Iowa.

Father David Hostetler

If I had planned from an early age to be an Orthodox Priest and U.S. Navy Chaplain, I couldn't have done a better job of preparing for it than God has done by prompting me to make choices that, at the time, I thought were my own ideas. These ideas often had nothing to do with either of those roles. Let me explain.

My father and grandfather were both ordained ministers in a Protestant church. Both of my father's brothers were also, at one time or another, church pastors. My own brother also accepted a calling into ordained ministry. Being a pastor was our family business, and as my father's oldest son, I was expected to follow in his footsteps. This I knew I couldn't do. For reasons I now recognize as selfish, I opted to enter the workforce to earn a living that I could use to give generously to the church. I thought God was calling me to do that, because I believed I had a high earning potential. So I joined the Navy. The training the Navy would provide me at no cost (save an eight-year service commitment) would allow me to make a comfortable living when I finished my service. This was the idea, and my first choice.

I was sincere in seeking God's will and plan for me, and that the choice I made was what He wanted, but I know my parents didn't think so. Had I not joined the Navy, though, I would not have met the young Greek woman who captured my heart. Not only was she Greek, she was Orthodox, with a sincerity that only grew after we were married. In anticipation of the arrival of our first son, I knew I had to make a decision to unify the faith in our home, and I knew by then that my wife wasn't going to shift in my Protestant direction. As I explored Orthodoxy and began to understand that my misgivings were based on misunderstandings, my heart began to open to another prompting of the Holy Spirit. I was received into the Orthodox Church in August of 2000, three months before our first son was born.

By this time, I had served my eight years of enlisted service in the submarine force and was working in the private sector. I was earning a comfortable living that allowed my wife to concentrate on raising our children, and we were, as I'd promised God, giving as generously as we could to the Church and other charities. The problem was that I hated my job. So I made another choice and started to go to night school to get a college degree. My employer covered the costs, provided I followed one of three specific degree paths. I picked business management and was on my way.

In the years following my reception into the Orthodox Church, I felt my first calling as a prompting to join the choir where I enjoyed participating more directly in worship. Then the protopsaltis called me to help with chanting and reading at the psaltiri. I even began to help in the altar—especially during weekday liturgies that I was able to attend because of my rotating shift work. Little by little I found that the place where I felt most fulfilled, and for which I was most properly suited, was in church helping the priest.

I told my wife that I was thinking about being a priest. Her response was prompt: "I wondered how long it would take you to figure that out." She had known all along. When I told my priest that I thought I was being called to the priesthood, he told me not to rush it. "If God wants you, you won't be able to get away." That's the advice I got most often when I asked how to know if I was truly being called to the priesthood. But what does that mean? What does it look like? What does it feel like when God chases you down?

I was still early enough in my degree program that, though still in business management, I could focus my research on church-related matters and graduate on time. I was still uncertain about being a priest, still miserable with my job, and worried that I was choosing to be a priest only because I wanted out of my job. I made another decision and applied for a job on the East Coast. When they made me an offer, I had to make another difficult choice between going to seminary on the one hand, and going to a new job on the other. This was another moment where God intervened.

It happened that my uncle visited while I was mulling this over. Over conversation at dinner, I mentioned that I was considering a job on the East Coast but wasn't certain I should take it. "Why not?" he asked, forcing me to share what had been until then a closely guarded secret—that I was considering becoming a priest. He was quiet for a moment and then gave me the best perspective I'd heard yet about the topic.

"David," he said, "I don't know anything about the priesthood, but this I can say without reservation: if you can get away from entering ordained ministry, then stay out of it."

The veil lifted. This was a perspective I could use. If I took that other job, I would wonder for the rest of my life if I had made the right choice. If I went to seminary and found that to be a huge mistake, I could always find another job. I would never be able to get away from ministry without giving it a try first. It had already haunted me for most of my life.

We sold our house and moved to Boston. After settling in and getting started, I felt that for the first time in my life, I was exactly where I was supposed to be. Not because it was easy; it wasn't. In addition to the work of spiritual formation, chapel attendance, and completing my degree program, I had to provide for my growing family. (We had two more sons while there, bringing our total to four.) I remember being tired for most of the four years I was at Holy Cross, but I would do it all again without a second thought. No, it felt right because God had been preparing me for this for my entire life. I even used skills I learned in the Navy while I was there.

When I started my seminary training, I had only really expected to become a parish priest, but while I was there, I came to know a surprisingly large group of students who, like me, were veterans. Our group got together one evening to welcome a U.S. Navy Chaplain, Fr. Milton Gianulis. Looking sharp in his dress blues, Fr. Milton shared some sea stories and some of the joys and benefits of military service in the chaplain corps. What struck me as curious was that he said he'd been a reservist. I didn't think a priest could serve in the reserves. How could he serve one weekend a month with his parish responsibilities? So, I asked him. After learning the details, I still didn't think the reserves were the way to go. I wasn't so happy with my prior service in the Navy that I was eager to put on a uniform again. The idea went onto the back burner, almost forgotten.

But the idea was persistent enough that I shared it with my closest friends at seminary. We had gotten into the habit of checking in with each other regularly, and we were in the car headed to dinner when I mentioned that after Fr. Milton's talk I had been thinking about joining the Navy Chaplain Corps. Without hesitation, all three of them said nearly in unison, "you need to do that." Not liking to be told what to do, however, I gave them all of my very good reasons to not do that—including that I had already done that and didn't like it. To end the discussion, I agreed to mention the idea to my bishop, expecting he would take my side and want me in a parish.

I called the Metropolis a couple days later and told the bishop that I was thinking about joining the Navy Chaplain Corps and why. Not only did he NOT take my side, he told me he thought that was a great idea and perfect for me. As it turns out he was right, for reasons neither he nor I had any way of knowing at the time, though God certainly did. He had been preparing me for this my entire life.

Having been brought up in a Protestant Church I can easily understand and communicate with most of the Christians in the Navy and its Chaplain Corps. With my prior enlisted service, I have a more intimate understanding of what our sailors's lives are like than is otherwise possible. Even though I am an Orthodox priest—one of such a small number that there are more Jewish rabbis in the fleet— serving one of the smallest Christian communities in the military, the importance of being in places like Afghanistan or on a deployed ship to offer the sacraments to Orthodox Christians who otherwise would have to do without is a blessing of inestimable value to them and to me.

God knew what he was doing with my life long before I had any clue what He was doing. I certainly couldn't even have imagined this work or this life when I was a young man. I also could never have recognized the Lord's calling without the help of trusted friends and mentors. From my own meager perspective I might never have seen it. But God knew that too, which is why He gave my advisors to me.

I have no idea what God has planned for me from this point on, but I've learned that as long as I continue to seek His will and make my choices with that end in mind, and to seek guidance from the men whose perspective I have come to trust, even if I make a wrong turn, He will still get me to where He wants me to be. And when I get there, He will have equipped me to the job.

Fr. David Hostetler serves in the U.S. Navy Chaplain Corps
and is currently the Deputy Command Chaplain
for U.S. Naval Support Activity, Naples, Italy

Father Andrew Karamitos

How did my calling to the priesthood come to be? It was, November 30, 1971, the feast day of St. Andrew. We had just moved to New Jersey from Delaware, where I was born nine months earlier. My late mother was a pious and devout Orthodox Christian who had instilled in my sister and me to live a Christ-centered life. The faith was first—then other things.

My mother was always the first to be at church for any worship service. The running joke was that she had to be there before the priest to unlock the door. We would always ask her, show us the key.

So, on this day, the feast day of St. Andrew, after receiving my excused absence from school, we sat in church, first pew as always, and we waited for Father to invoke, "Blessed is our God..." to start Orthros. As I sat there watching, I remember Fr. Socrates Tsamustalis turning around and looking at me from altar and pointing to call me to the solea. Not knowing what was happening, shear panic came upon me. "Did I do something wrong?" He kept motioning for me to come, and the more he motioned, the more I wanted to run out the back door.

Mom stood me up and joyfully pushed me towards the altar. It was the longest walk of my life, but it was a walk that brought me to the holy priesthood. I recall my mom saying to me when Church finished, "Did you like serving as an altar boy?" I did, and it was an amazing experience. I remember to this day looking at everything behind the altar, and being curious as to what everything was, and what Fr. Socrates was doing. I saw the swinging of the censor and how only the captains touched it. I hoped one day I would be able to hold it and walk with it during the Great Entrance. I looked forward to serving as an altar boy every Sunday and being among the older altar boys. I wanted to be the first at church; I wanted to have the key to unlock the door.

As the years passed, and I became an altar boy captain, I was folding Father's vestments to put them away. I was curious to see what the epitrachelion (stole) would look like on me. I went back and forth in my head; no was around—should I put it around my neck? Should I not? Well, I did, only for a brief second. Low and behold, Father turned the corner and looked at me. The same fear that came upon me as when he pointed at me to come to the solea came upon me again. I apologized and begged for forgiveness. He smiled at me and said in a gentle voice, "So what did you feel?" Not understanding what he meant, I stood there frozen, in fear he would be upset. He knew that I was speechless. He saw I was trembling. Yet in his fatherly voice, asked me, "Would you like to be a priest?" And there it happened, for the first time, I had said yes.

For the next two years, Father took me under his mentorship! He allowed me to do more things within the church—far more than serving as an altar boy. I worked in the church office and joined him on his pastoral visits to feed the hungry. Each moment, each day in the church, gave me such joy and grew my conviction that I wanted to serve the church as one of Christ's priests.

My senior year came, and I had received the Hellenic College application. I filled it out and placed it in the mail. The final thing I needed was the letter from my parish priest to be filled out. I brought it to him. I will never forget the tears that fell from his eyes as he looked at me and said, "This is one of my highlights in my priesthood, I say to you Andrea. Go and answer the calling of our Lord."

To this day, I wake up every morning hearing Father's words, "Go and answer the calling of the Lord."

My calling is simple; I became a priest due to a powerful mentor and spiritual father, prayer, study, and discernment. I believe this is who God called me to be. While I had to overcome my own selfishness and learn to trust the Lord, once I changed the question from "What do I want to do when I grow up?" to "who is God calling me to be?" I have found great peace in following God's call to the priesthood. While I know my life will not always be easy or feel fulfilling, I know God has called me to the priesthood and by faithfully living out that call to the priesthood, God will bring me immense joy and peace.

Father Andrew Karamitos serves at
Saint Sophia Church in Elgin, Illinois.

Father Achilles Karathanos

Whenever I am asked whether I was raised in the Church or if I am a convert to Orthodoxy, my answer is simply, "Yes." Allow me to explain. My father, Demetrius, came to the United States from Greece as a young immigrant with the goal of furthering his education. Living with his uncle, Achilles, in southern Illinois, he was eventually able to enroll in university, acquire an engineering degree, and ultimately become a professor of quantitative analysis. While teaching college algebra as an assistant, my father was endeared to one of his students, Patricia Hager, who was retaking the course after having previously dropped it at another school. The endearment was mutual and led to Mr. and Mrs. Karathanos uniting in the Sacrament of Marriage in Montreal, Canada, a few years later.

Together they raised me, my brother, and sister in a most loving and caring manner. Yet, due to geographic and other circumstances, they practically abandoned Orthodox Christianity in the process.

My Mother and her siblings grew up in a household headed by parents who shared the Christian faith and values, but who maintained fidelity to two very different traditions throughout their adult lives. My Grandfather, Floyd, was of German stock, an Air Force officer and veteran, an educator in agriculture, and a deacon of the Southern Baptist Church. My Grandmother, Mary, was the child of Ukrainian immigrants and was baptized and raised as a devout Orthodox Christian. In their household of five children, Floyd and Mary were able to maintain a well-run and united home despite attending their different churches every Sunday throughout their lives. All the children were baptized Orthodox but meandered between traditions without fully embracing one or the other.

What did that mean for me and my siblings? At the insistence of my grandmother, Anthi, in Greece, my brother, Nikolas and I were baptized on the same day on a family trip to Greece. He was two, and I was one. My sister, Katya, was baptized on another trip to Greece, around the age of twelve.

My siblings and I were all raised in a small university town in southern Missouri, where there was no Orthodox Church. As a family, we simply didn't attend church. Yet I wholeheartedly believe and trust that the beginning of my calling to the priesthood and ministry was engendered in the simple faith of my yiayia, Anthi, who insisted upon my baptism. "For as many of you as were baptized into Christ have put on Christ" (Gal. 3:27).

A deposit of grace was bestowed and received. It wasn't nurtured in a traditional manner, but my mother taught me to pray. I prayed often as an adolescent and teenager to an "unknown God," and my heart was open to things of the spirit. This openness of heart allowed me to enter a "faith journey," where ultimately, I was seeking the person of Christ and looking for truth—the truth that would set me free (Jn. 8:32).

This journey included attending a Southern Baptist-affiliated undergraduate school, where I met my future Presvytera, Yianna. Presv. Yianna—at that time, Usha—had parents who were East Indian immigrants. Her parents were Christian, but not unlike my grandparents, combined a mix of Protestant and Orthodox (Malankara Syrian Orthodox) upbringings.

While my course of studies was primarily secular in nature (Institutions and Policy, and Spanish), studying at a Christian school opened to me opportunities to study the Scriptures and, probably more important at that time of my formation, opportunities to serve others. I participated in two Habitat for Humanity house-building mission trips in rural Texas and in Guatemala. My eyes were opened to the wider world we shared with many who suffered and struggled for sustenance on a daily basis. A deep, yet unguided, conviction was growing in my heart to use the talents and education I had received to serve God and my fellow brothers and sisters.

Thus, when the well-known Evangelical speaker and writer, Tony Campolo, visited my college a few months before I graduated, I had no qualms heeding his call to give "two months of our lives" to serve underprivileged kids of the streets of Camden, New Jersey. An organization he founded, Urban Promise, offered free summer camps infused with the Gospel of Christ to kids who likely had never experienced anything outside of their immediate urban surroundings.

Both Usha and I went to Camden that summer for a two-month commitment that very quickly turned into two years. We stayed on as urban youth worker interns, who continued our education on issues of urban poverty and racial disparity, and we helped develop and run after-school tutoring and youth ministry programs. We lived in a communal staff house in the heart of North Camden, and my whiteness stuck out like a sore thumb. Some of the kids knew of the Italians over in Philly and figured I must be one of them.

Ministering to the youth and their families during those two years in Camden was pivotal for my internally developing call to serve. I was constantly stretched beyond my own ability and talents so that I learned to weep and rely on God. I witnessed deep joys and sorrows of families that were struggling to maintain food and shelter. One family had lived with the "plumbing" of two buckets in their bathroom and a back alley in which to dump. A young teenager by the name of Eddie had graduated from our camp programs and was working as a street leader with the organization. Eddie invited my colleague, John, and I over to dinner at his mom's. Evidently his mother—a single mother—struggled with mental illness, but she seemed overjoyed and proud to have us over for spaghetti. When Eddie had John and me sit down and enjoy the meal, we asked if they would join us. Eddie said they would, but they would wait until we finished because they had to wash their only two plates and utensils first.

During this intense time of inner-city youth ministry in Camden, I felt that I needed an outlet for stress-relief and personal development, so I began to pursue study of Modern Greek. I found a personal tutor in Cherry Hill, New Jersey, who not only instructed me in Greek, but invited me to events at her parish. Ultimately, I attended Holy Pascha services there at St. Thomas Greek Orthodox Church, and I was mystified with a sense of holiness and wonder. I knew very little of Holy Orthodoxy or the history of the Church, but the seed was planted.

From Camden, I returned to Kansas City, where I had a network of friends from college. I began working retail in a friend's family business, but my mind was on things from on high. For a while, I continued attending an Evangelical church literally called I.H.O.P. No, they didn't serve pancakes; it was an acronym for International House of Prayer. I also arranged a seeker's meeting with Fr. Charles Sarelis, the proistamenos at the Annunciation Greek Orthodox Church. Essentially, like any good priest would, he invited me to "come and see." I began attending the Divine Liturgy on occasion, and while I experienced the same beauty and mystery as I did at Holy Pascha, I felt that there was something missing. This perception likely had just as much do with me as the parish. As it was a well to do suburban parish, I sensed a disconnect with the worship and the parish's mission to the world. Carrying deep in my bosom my experience in Camden, I was looking for a church that was directly involved in serving the poor and outcasts.

As providence would have it, some friends I had made in a "Pauline Epistles" study group from the I.H.O.P. informed me of a fervent and compassionate Orthodox priest who served a parish in the heart of the city. It turned out I was only living five blocks from this St. Mary of Egypt Orthodox Church, located at 3101 Troost Ave., the historic racial dividing line of the city. At that time, Fr. Paisius and Matushka Michaela Altschul were not only leading a fervent and robust liturgical life, but they were also evangelizing and serving both the rich and the poor, the stable, and the demonized and distraught, and were outreaching to a neighborhood that was in much distress. After one or two visits, I knew I had found home.

While I had been reading some history and theology of the Church, now I was experiencing the fullness of Christianity—that for which my heart had long pined—on a day-to-day basis. I got permission to leave work fifteen minutes early to attend daily vespers. I religiously attended the Saturday All-Night Vigil (Russian tradition) and partook of regular confession in preparation to receive the Holy Gifts. In short, I became a small sponge, trying to soak up the vast ocean of Holy Orthodoxy, and I couldn't get enough.

With the blessing of Fr. Paisius, who received me as a spiritual son, I saved up and embarked on a pilgrimage across the western states, visiting every Orthodox monastery I could find. I spent a week at St. Anthony's in Arizona, but my final destination was the St. Herman of Alaska Monastery in Platina, California. There I spent most of Great Lent, Holy Week, Pascha, and Bright Week, and I returned home to Kansas City spiritually renewed and burning as a bright candle in my love for God and for the mission of the Church.

While I had to settle back into life in the world and renew my responsibilities to my employer, my parish community, family, and friends, I felt that I had been gifted an inner fire that could not be extinguished. Whatever I would do with my life would be for the love of God and His Church. The words of Elder Thaddeus of Vitovnica resonate with the state of being I experienced: "Even as a child I greatly desired to serve God. Even then I knew that here on earth everything was some kind of service. Parents attend to their children and children to their parents. Everyone serves someone else. That was when I decided that I wanted to serve God. Since He is the parent of all mankind and the entire universe, one should serve Him Who is the greatest of all" (Our Thoughts Determine our Lives, St. Herman Press, p. 91).

While I had an inkling that one day this desire to serve could possibly take on the form of ordination and the priesthood, I recognized that I was but an infant nursing on spiritual milk and could not yet even think about solid meat. For the next four to five years, I simply "put my hand to the plow" and did my utmost to make a living, to be faithful to Christ and those whom God placed in my path, and to prayerfully see where that would lead.

During that time, through our friendship and conversations, and by the moving of the Spirit, my close friend, Usha, also became a catechumen in the faith. Our paths converged and we began a serious courtship. In retrospect, I am greatly humbled at how greatly respectful and immensely patient Usha was with me and with our relationship.

Desiring to keep absorbing the grace I had experienced the previous Lent, I arranged to spend the next Lenten season in Greece on pilgrimage to several monasteries. I was most fortunate and blessed to be received for most of Great Lent as a pilgrim at the St. Andrew Kelli (a dependency of the Great Lavra) on the Holy Mountain. This is not the time and place to describe the wonders I experienced there, but suffice it to say I departed satiated: "Thou anointest my head with oil; my cup runneth over!" (Ps. 23:5)

I was becoming more and more grounded, anchored in faith, and united to Christ. I was also not so subtly reminded by my dear Usha that it was time to make a decision. This last pilgrimage had been a time for inner discernment. Would I possibly become a monastic? As beautiful and spiritually bountiful as I witnessed the monastic life to be, I was also satisfied to learn that I was not made for it. By God's grace, I was now certain that I desired marriage, and I was ready to commit to Usha. Thanks be to God, so was she to me!

Usha, who received the name Yianna (after St. John the Dwarf) in baptism, and I were married by Fr. Paisius in June of 1999. We took an "alternative" honeymoon, where we spent a week or two traveling through the southwestern states and landed at the St. Paisius Missionary School (at the St. Paisius Monastery in California), where Yianna stayed with the women in the monastery, and I slept on a cot in a garage with other male pilgrims and students for the next three weeks! We took to heart the symbol of the newly- crowned couple's first steps in marriage being led by the Gospel of Christ!

We returned to Kansas City where Yianna took up teaching in a Catholic school, and I returned where I had left off learning the trade of automotive technician. We purchased a little house on the edge of the city, devoted ourselves to Church life, and started raising a family. Our first child, Demetrius, was born on April 27th, 2000, and was an indescribable joy. It was during this time in our lives that the latent "seed" and thought of seminary began to sprout. I had moved on from two automotive service positions to a job in an industrial machine shop for hydraulic valves, and while it paid the bills, there was no future in it. Yianna had left teaching and was now a full-time mother and homemaker. In conversations with Fr. Paisius, he blessed me to go and see the Orthodox seminaries, and, if it felt right, to apply. Circumstances not only developed to allow us to go to seminary but seemed to push us in that direction.

In the Spring of 2001, I flew out east and visited both St. Tikhon's Seminary in Pennsylvania and Holy Cross in Brookline, Massachusetts.

While St. Tikhon's had a certain peaceful and spiritual allure, one great drawback was that they had no married student housing, and rentals were hard to come by in the immediate vicinity. I couldn't imagine leaving Yianna and little Demetri in an isolated apartment everyday while I spent my days at the seminary. I then visited Holy Cross in Brookline. My parish, St. Mary of Egypt, was in the Serbian Archdiocese of America, and so I didn't have a particular attachment to any of the seminaries by jurisdiction. I didn't know a single soul in all of Boston. At least I didn't think I did. Upon attending a few classes as a prospective student, I was thrilled to see Bogomil, one of my "honeymoon" garage roommates from the missionary school studying at Holy Cross. We caught up a little, and I got his perspective on things. I was also humbled by some of the loving hospitality of other students I met. There was true joy on campus.

The next great obstacle was financial. When I visited the Office of Student Aid, the director asked me if I had applied for the Leadership 100 Scholarship for seminarians. I told her that I wasn't in the Greek Archdiocese, and that I wasn't sure that it was applicable to someone in my situation. She assured me that it was. Within a very short time, I had applied and been accepted as a Leadership 100 Scholarship recipient! During that time, the scholarship covered full tuition and housing! I couldn't fathom God's unspeakable blessing and timing for this unworthy soul. I could believe, and I did believe, in His calling on my life. That calling was to train, to be formed, and to ultimately serve as His priest. "A man's heart plans his way, but the Lord directs his steps" (Prov. 16:9).

By the time I graduated from Holy Cross in 2005, I had received the blessing of my bishop, His Grace, Bishop Longin of New Gracanica, as well as the blessing of the Chancellor of the Greek Orthodox Archdiocese of America—at that time, His Grace, Bishop Sava—to be ordained in the Greek Orthodox Archdiocese of America.

I had been petitioning His Grace, Bishop Sava, as well as Metropolitan Isaiah of Denver, to first serve as a missionary priest in Albania, with the plan to return to the Holy Metropolis of Denver at His Eminence's discretion. While I was patiently waiting for a communication on this request, I received the heavy news that my father, Demetrius, was diagnosed with an aggressive form of lung cancer. Upon prayerful consideration, I withdrew my application for Albania, with the hope to be ordained and serve in a community nearer to the home of my parents in southern Missouri. The Metropolis of Denver had no openings. A seminary brother put me in touch with the Chancellor of the Metropolis of Chicago, who told me that, in fact, the proistamenos of St. Nicholas Greek Orthodox Church in St. Louis, Missouri, was seeking an associate priest to aid in the parish's vast ministries. St. Nicholas is 116 miles from my parent's home, with only one other Greek Orthodox parish slightly closer (by four miles)! Again, how could I not see God's hand guiding me forward?

Soon, I met with His Eminence, Metropolitan Iakovos, of beloved memory, who agreed to assign me as the assistant to Fr. Dionysios Papulis at St. Nicholas. First, I was ordained to the holy Diaconate by His Eminence, Metropolitan Isaiah, of Denver on June 12, 2005, at the Annunciation Greek Orthodox Church in Kansas City. I officially began serving at St. Nicholas in St. Louis, Missouri, on August 1st, 2005.

His Eminence, Metropolitan Iakovos, ordained me to the holy Priesthood on Sunday, November 6, 2005, at the culmination of the Metropolis of Chicago Clergy Laity Assembly, hosted by St. Nicholas in St. Louis. It just so happened that the day of my natural birth into this world—November 6th, 1971—coincided with my birth into the holy priesthood of our Lord and Savior Jesus Christ. "O Lord, how manifold are thy works! In wisdom hast thou made them all" (Psalm 104:24).

By God's Grace, my father lived another seven years on earth and came to know and love not only his namesake, Demetrius, but our other three children, Isadora, Samuel, and Isaac. By God's mercy, I was able to spend joyous days with him and serve him as both his son and priest. May God grant that my continued serving in the priesthood of our Lord Jesus Christ bear witness and testimony to his loving fatherhood and to the honor of my mother who taught me to pray. Dearest father, Demetri, Papa, may your repose be blessed and your memory eternal. Amen.

Τέλος και τω Θεώ Δόξα!

Father Achilles Karathanos serves at
Saints Constantine and Helen Church in Swansea, Illinois.

Father Chris Kerhulas

I grew up on the West Side of Chicago. I went to Plato Elementary School on Harrison and Central Street. I graduated from Plato in June 1963, and went to Austin High School from fall, 1963 until I graduated in June 1967. I went to Hellenic College from 1967 until graduation in 1971; then, on to Holy Cross Greek Orthodox School of Theology from 1971 through graduation with a Master of Divinity in June 1974. I married Maria Stathopoulos, whom I met in Denver in May of 1975. We had two children, Georgia and Peter, and now have three granddaughters, Ava Marissa, and Vincentia.

I served as associate pastor of St. Nicholas Greek Orthodox Church in Oak Lawn, IL, from 1975-78. I was pastor of St. Demetrios Greek Orthodox Church in Waukegan, IL, from 1978-1981. I then worked for the Metropolis of Chicago in 1981 serving as Youth Director for the Midwest. I also took over the inner-city church of St. Basil in 1981 on Ashland and Polk Street, in the West Loop area. I held both positions through 1989, when I terminated my tenure as youth director, but continued at St. Basil until July 2010. During the entire period of 1981 through 2010 I served on numerous national youth commissions and various national clergy activist organizations. This included a two-year term as national president of our clergy association, representing over 600 clergymen called the Archdiocese Presbyters Council. I authored a book called Parent Points, which is based on my experiences with young people and parents.

I was also in three independent films. "Do You Wanna Dance?" was released in 1996 and was based on my ministry, life, and philosophies. This grew out of my relationship with filmmaker Robert Krantz (Karountzos).

One of my proudest involvements was four years at the Ionian Village summer camp program on the western coast of Greece, beginning in 1983. Young people still participate in this incredible, life-changing program to this day. I retired from the active ministry in July 2010 but still help at St. Nectarios Greek Orthodox Church in Palatine, IL.

My growing up within the Church's umbrella always kept me turning to our Faith throughout the difficult phases of development. Because of all the gifts my young life was blessed with, the power and strength of growing directed me to always asking how to "give back!"

Loving through serving led me to the challenge of turning to my mentor and confessor The Very Rev. Kallistos Samaras, as to where my life should go. The Seminary (Hellenic College) let me in at 17 years of age to begin answering that question of where my life should proceed. Seven incredible years at Hellenic College and Holy Cross gave me the space and opportunity to answer Christ's call. As my mind questioned, my heart embraced! It was bringing Christ to the hearts of the people Christ put into my life and ministry.

Father Chris Kerhulas is a retired priest who serves at St Nectarios Church in Palatine, Illinois.

Father Chrysanthos Kerkeres

The Letter to the Hebrews says that, when it comes to the priesthood, "no one takes this honor upon himself but only when called by God" (Heb. 5:4). The priesthood is indeed not a job, but a life of service and requires a special calling.

I was very much an ordinary child that grew up in an immigrant home. My parents emigrated from Greece, and they worked very hard to raise their children to have a better life than they had. However, the most precious inheritance that we received from our parents was not financial, rather it was the treasure of the Orthodox faith.

My earliest memories of childhood include my parents telling me biblical stories. My parents lived the faith in our home. We learned to pray, to fast, and to participate in the Holy Sacraments, not only because they told us to, but because we watched how they lived.

As I entered my teenage years, I spent most every Sunday and every major feast day attending the Divine Liturgy. Our church became our home! By the time I entered high school, I found myself at church four or five days a week. I was not only attending services, but I was involved in the parish youth programs, athletics, etc.

Many years of involvement in our church led to moments that I cannot fully explain, but that I can only assume were God calling me to serve His Church. I would experience this unexplainable desire to learn more about the Church, and I would feel an incredible comfort and warmth during the divine services. No matter how much I would tell myself that I was not worthy to serve Christ as a priest, somehow, it seemed that I could not fully escape the thought.

For me, the call to serve was not a specific miraculous moment, but rather many moments and events over many years. It was encounters with people, like our parish priest who was able to bring Christ to us in simple and exciting ways; it was the monk I met on Mount Athos who looked at a group of us and said as if he were thinking out loud, "This one is going to be a priest." Mostly, it was seeing humble and dedicated clergy who served Christ and His Church with all their heart, soul, and strength. I watched as these wonderful priests comforted the sad, celebrated with the joyous, and most importantly, I watched how they worked to bring people closer to Christ to save their souls.

I believe that the call to serve as a priest comes from God. Christ called Peter, Andrew, James, and John, and Paul. He called each one individually, and he called them by name. It was not their choice. Each apostle was unworthy, but Jesus called him anyway. If I discerned correctly all those years ago, I guess I to was called to serve by God, and I am blessed to serve His Church in spite of my unworthiness as long as He allows.

Father Chrysanthos Kerkeres serves at Saint George Church in Chicago, Illinois.

Father John Ketchum

I have always had a close connection with the Greek Orthodox Church. My mother's first cousin was Presvytera Olga Psillas, so I called her husband Rev. Protopresbyter John Psillas, my "uncle" out of respect. He played a special role in my life, beginning with my baptism and thankfully being able to bless the wedding rings at my engagement to my wife, Veronica.

Growing up in New Jersey and then Ft. Pierce, Florida, I always served as an altar boy in church. The priest at St. Nicholas Church in Florida at the time was Fr. John Liadis. He also ran the diocese youth camp during the summer in Brooksville, Florida. One year, he enticed the altar boys with a free trip to Disney World for whoever would attend every Holy Week service. I enthusiastically attended each Holy Week service with the Disney trip dangled in front of me; however, along the way, a seed was planted for a real appreciation for the beauty and meaning of our Orthodox services.

I continued to serve as an altar boy through my senior year of high school, and every summer I would attend the diocese summer camp with Fr. John. The camp was very simple and had very basic accommodation. At first, the chapel was an outdoor A-frame structure, but by the time I finished high school, they had built a regular indoor chapel with an altar. This little chapel was also dedicated to St. Nicholas, and it was in this tiny chapel that I would later have a significant encounter with the Lord. Attending this camp each summer really started to cement my learning and love for our Orthodox Christian faith.

The Greek Orthodox Camp was also a part of my life during my college years. I would return each summer to serve on staff as a counselor. I attended the University of Central Florida, majoring in political science and international relations. UCF also had an Air Force ROTC program that became part of my career plan. I was to enter the Air Force as a commissioned officer after graduation. Before I could begin Air Force officer's basic training, I had to pass a battery of tests. First, I had to pass the most difficult test I had ever taken, the Air Force Officer Qualifying Test (AFOQT). The test itself is very demanding. It had 550 test items divided into 12 unique sections and two main areas: verbal analogies and arithmetic reasoning. This test started in the morning, broke for lunch, and you completed it by the early evening. I was happy to have made the cut with a passing score, yet still had to pass a physical fitness test, a psychological evaluation, and dental and medical exams.

All things were going well, until I received some bad news from the eye doctor. He told me I had glaucoma, a group of eye diseases that can cause vision loss and blindness by damaging the optic nerve. Unfortunately, this eye condition would cancel any potential officer commission in the Air Force. In the blink of an eye, all my plans for the future were shattered and had to change. It felt like a punch in the gut, and I was very upset and confused. I didn't know what to do, so I drove to the Orthodox summer camp where I had spent so many summers of my young life. The camp was not in session yet, but I entered the little chapel of St. Nicholas and started to pray.

Something drew me forward, and I then felt the need to go inside the altar. As I was going to go through the north door to enter the holy altar, which traditionally has the icon of the Archangel Michael, the icon of the Archangel fell off the icon screen! That really startled me, and I quickly tried to put it back in place, and then I entered the holy altar. All of sudden all my anxiety about what I was going to do with my life went away and I felt an overwhelming feeling of calm and peace. I can say that was the moment when I received my calling to the priesthood. A voice came to me saying this is where you belong. I had a feeling that this is where my home was; this is where I was supposed to be, to serve inside the altar. Now, after this chaotic and confusing time, I realized what I was going to do with my life. I had always enjoyed serving the Church as an altar boy and at summer camp but serving as a priest in the Church had never even crossed my mind until that very moment. I then spoke with Fr. John Liadis and my parish priest in Orlando, Fr. Michael Kontogiorgis, and they assisted me in applying to Holy Cross Greek Orthodox School of Theology. I then drove to my mother's home and told her I had made a major career change. Before I had the chance to tell her my news she stopped in her tracks, turned around and told me straight out, "You are going to become a priest." I was in total shock, and I asked her how she knew this already. She said, "God just spoke to me and told me."

After being accepted to Holy Cross, I went to visit the campus and sat in on couple of classes and was really looking forward to beginning my master's degree program after graduation. I still had one semester more to complete and attended Holy Trinity parish in Orlando while at school. I attended the Holy Week services that year, 1991, with even greater attention. If I might have still had some lingering doubt about my calling to the priesthood, it was even more solidified that Pascha night. I know that I experienced the power of the Holy Spirit. The Church was completely darkened, and the royal doors to the altar shut (as this parish had a sliding door that closed off the altar). When the door opened just before midnight at singing of the hymn, "Come Receive the Light" and with the emergence of the phos (light) from the holy altar, I felt the inexpressible power of the Holy Spirit. It is somewhat indescribable, except to say it was like an invisible torrent of energy, somewhat like a wave of water flowing that poured out and hit me so hard, that for a split second time seemed to stand still, and I was overwhelmed with joy and the power and energy of the living God. It was from that day forward that I truly understood what my calling to the priesthood meant, and that God is truly real, and the power of God exists. This is why I am so passionate about our Orthodox faith, and why every liturgy, for me, has great meaning.

This is not the end of the story of my calling to the priesthood. After graduation, but before entering Holy Cross, I received a letter from the Air Force saying that my eye exam was in error,and that I did not have glaucoma after all! This was confirmed with subsequent eye exams. I could not believe it! I was offered my commission to the Air Force officer's basic training which I turned down. That settled it for me; I knew then that I was meant to be a priest and not to serve as an officer in the Air Force. This truly confirmed that the path to the holy priesthood was for me, and it fostered in me a serious approach to my studies. I graduated from Holy Cross School Greek Orthodox of Theology with my Master of Divinity in 1995. I was ordained a deacon in June 1996 and a priest in July 1996. Glory to God for all things!

Father John Ketchum serves at
Kimissis Tis Theotokou Church in Racine, Wisconsin.

Father Demetrios Kounavis

I suppose most of us have early memories of going to church—of that warm and beautiful place with paintings and comfortable long pews, where one could lay with a pacifier and sleep while the people gathered finely dressed to sing and say prayers. It was God's house. I would turn and run away when the nice old church ladies tried to pinch my cheeks and give me attention. While I may have been fidgety in my pew as a youngster, I still liked to go. I appreciated it. I just didn't realize how much until I got older and started making my own decisions about how I would spend my day.

I was an energetic child that lived close enough to the church to walk—or rather speed walk— there and to my elementary school, which was across the street from the church, every day. I was active in the church programs and was familiar with the layout of the parish grounds. One day as a little child, during a Vespers service with many people in church and me in my pew, I remember being jealous seeing one of my friends serving in the holy altar, wearing a beautiful golden altar boy robe and holding a stick with a red glass at the top. I said to myself that I wanted to do that too. Alas, I found out that I was still too young to assume those responsibilities and buried the thought of being an altar boy for a later day.

At eleven years old, my first experience as an altar boy was to have the priest grab me by the arm and escort me back out of the royal gates, sternly telling me to never go through those doors again. I had approached the associate priest at the time and asked to become an altar boy. He said to come on Sunday to church for liturgy. I made sure I was early, and the service had not started yet. That was when I learned the first rule of being an altar boy—only a priest can go through the royal gates and stand in front of the holy altar table. Since that time, I had almost never missed a Sunday liturgy serving in the altar. Neither he nor I could have known that less than twenty years later, I would be escorted by each arm to pass through those same gates to receive Holy Ordination by the laying on of hands.

The church was a large part of my life growing up. Greek school was held three days a week back then. I attended many fruitful and formative youth programs. I felt the church and I were connected since my friends and I basically lived there and had explored every nook and cranny of the enormous facility. I was also in Sunday school, which I cut regularly to stay serving in the altar. At a seminarian scholarship interview with our Sunday school director, she asked me why I wouldn't go to class. Jokingly, I half lowered my head in shame, and she said she understood where my calling was; I got the scholarship.

When possible, Lenten services and Holy Week, along with the weekday and other services were added to my attendance schedule. I remember one year, in a dark church, silent in anticipation, with incense burning, candlelight flickering and reflecting off of golden vessels, the priest carrying the crucified Christ at the service of the Twelve Gospels service and singing alone with the deepest lament, and me holding the same candle stick with the red glass at the top. It moved the whole church, including me. to weep. I think that is when the Lord inspired me to pursue a life of service in the Church, but not in any specific way yet, I loved serving and singing along from inside the beautiful holy altar. As the years went by, I persisted in my service and also had a new, strong desire to help the chanters at the psaltiri. They started me off with reading and singing along with the melodies with which I was familiar.

Church music moved my soul. I was led to start studying Byzantine chant. This is the time when the fire of the desire to become a priest consumed me. My vision of life became crystal clear. I was standing at my spot at the psaltiri one day and, like a hammer to the head, I made a connection to the antiquity of the Church and at the same time, God's eternal presence. It was a strong mystical feeling pulling me towards worship. Music has shaped my priesthood as well.

Chanting is a great part of worship and can inspire people to come closer to God. Chanting and worshiping with God's people felt like paradise, because that is what church is when we come together.

I received encouragement from all directions. With the example of influential clergy, the blessing of my spiritual father, the blessing of the bishop, and with the full support of my family, I decided to apply to and attend theological school with the intention of studying for the priesthood. Once I graduated from high school, I stayed near home for initial university studies and two years later, transferred to Hellenic College to complete my undergraduate degree. I felt great joy when I was accepted into Holy Cross to complete my graduate studies as a seminarian. Upon graduation, I had a whirlwind year. I was married in July, ordained a deacon in October, and ordained a priest in January. I give glory to God for all the blessings and challenges He helped me overcome all these years since my youth, and I pray that the Lord inspires future clergymen to take on this most divine vocation.

Father Demetrios Kounavis serves at
St George Church in Schererville, Indiana.

Father Nichalas March

There are many ways to be a teacher!

This is how my calling to the priesthood began: it was a very simple encounter that even at that time seemed surreal to me. These simple words initiated my call, but that call was not a simple process for me. It was not like the call of the Prophet Isaiah, who heard the words and responded,

"Here I am, God, send me!" (Isa. 6:8). It was a call with several steps and components in it that all had to be met in order for me to one day serve as a priest of our Lord's Holy Church. It was a journey into a truly new life, both in Christ and in His Church.

I had always wanted to be a history teacher. After high school, I pursued my studies at the University of Illinois to accomplish that goal. During my sophomore year, I decided that I would engage in volunteer opportunities to strengthen my application to the teaching program in secondary education. I decided that I would help the protestant community that I belonged to at the time by teaching Sunday school. I taught Sunday school that year for that protestant community while I was studying at the university.

The day that my calling began was a Sunday afternoon—a Sunday afternoon no different than any other. That day after the Sunday service, the pastor of the community walked up to me and said, "There are many ways to be a teacher." I did not understand at that time what he was telling me. I am sure that my face expressed nothing but confusion. The pastor, on the other hand, who was an older retired man, seemed to have become youthful as he spoke those words. He held himself differently; his face expressed joy. The moment seemed to slow down, and the area behind him became white. Like a flash of lightning, though dazzling at the time, this surreal moment was over instantly after he finished saying those words. The pastor walked away and did not even wait for me to answer. Everything returned to normal, like nothing unusual had happened. The pastor began chatting with other people who also had attended the Sunday service that day. He never spoke to me again that day. I stood there wondering what had just happened.

What did his words mean? I had always wanted to be a teacher; what other kinds of teachers were there?

I had always known what I wanted to do in life since I was eleven years old. Now, that sense of certainty was shaken. I felt uneasy with these questions and began to wrestle with them. These questions were not something that I could let go of and forget.

I continued my life, but I could not go on with my life as it was until I answered these questions. I pursued my studies and took more classes. I found opportunities to help others as a volunteer summer school teaching assistant and as a volunteer at a local nursing home, organizing activities for the elderly. I still thought that I was engaging in all these activities to pad my application for the teaching program as I started my junior year at the University of Illinois, though something was changing inside of me. I was not thinking so much about myself and was starting to think more about others and how I could have a positive impact on their lives. I still wanted to be a teacher, because I loved history. I found myself enjoying both teaching and serving others, even though I was not teaching history. In this realization, I felt more and more at peace, but not entirely. What did it mean to seek other ways to be a teacher? Who else is a teacher? What did they teach?

On another day, while I was walking down the street on the way to class, I pondered what these words meant for my life. I stopped walking; I stood there frozen on the street. I looked around and my senses were heightened. Everything looked beautiful and smelled wonderful. I was by myself, but I did not feel alone. Who else is a teacher? A pastor is also a teacher. God was calling me to be a pastor to His people. I had my answer, but like Adam and Eve, I quickly realized that I was underdressed for the life that was now in front of me. I had never read through the Bible completely. Yes, I had attended worship services throughout most of my life, but I used to sneak out during the sermons because they were boring. What did I know about Christianity? I knew nothing about the subject that I was being called to teach. Even though I felt at peace, I was concerned about how I would communicate this calling to others. What would they say when I told them about my calling?

I began to construct a garment of fig leaves for myself. I decided that I would wait before I told anyone. I would use this time to challenge myself so I could know if this calling was real, then I would tell others about my calling to ministry and that I wanted to become a pastor. I thought, "I must at least read through the Bible once." I should also make a conscious decision to participate in the entirety of the Sunday services. Shortly afterwards, the pastor who had spoken those initial words to me left my community. I was not able to tell him at the time that I had received a calling to ministry.

I did tell the new leader who took over at my community about my calling to ministry. This person wanted me to become more involved in the wider organization that my community belonged to within the state of Illinois. Following this suggestion, I started attending all kinds of meetings. I quickly realized from these gatherings that I did not fit in with this group of people at all. They were very different in their beliefs and practices; many were actually Unitarian. They seemed willing to almost deny that Jesus was the Son of God to fit in better with society. I also began to understand that though these leaders preached unity out loud, deep down they really did not want to associate with people like me who held more traditional Christian beliefs. They wanted to change me or hoped that I would leave. I was not going to change—the true Christian beliefs had changed my life. I still wanted to become a pastor to teach, but to whom and where? This larger community that

I thought I belonged to did not want to hear the things that I had to teach. This particular group was leaving traditional Christian teachings behind; they did not want to listen. Who, out there, was still following traditional Christian teachings?

During my first read through the Bible, a passage from the Gospels had stuck in my mind, "not even the gates of Hell will prevail against the Church" (Matt. 16:18). I believed that this statement of our Lord was true. Having participated in all these gatherings, I began to ask myself, "Where was Christ's Church actually located today?" It had to exist up until our time, because the words of our Lord are true; it could not have ever ceased to exist. I decided that I needed to find where His Church was alive.

The third and final day, my calling came about because of my last reflection. Where was Christ's Church? I knew what God was calling me to do: to teach and to serve His people, His Church. I started to look for His people.

During my final year at the university, I began to apply what I had learned from my historical and philosophical studies to seek an answer to the question consuming my mind. I dove deep into the history and beliefs of all the Christian groups that I had ever encountered. Which one was Christ's Church? Who was still holding on to the teachings that Christ Himself had given to His apostles? Where had these apostolic teachings been handed down over time? Who still kept them and wanted to pass them down to future members of Christ's Church? I looked at various groups, but the groups always came up short. There was always some stumbling block, some part that just did not feel right. I ran into a dead end, and I did not know where to go from there. I knew that these groups were not the continuation of Christ's Church throughout the ages. Their beliefs and practices, and sometimes their very existence, had all come about after the apostolic times. The claims that they made were not true.

I intensified my prayer, in which I asked for divine help. Was I being too critical of these groups? Would I have to settle and be satisfied with the next best thing? These were questions that I asked myself while also praying for divine wisdom.

I was graduating soon. I had been accepted into a protestant seminary, but I knew that I could not become a pastor, a teacher, or a servant of that group. What was I going to do? While I was struggling with this dilemma, the very same pastor who had spoken the words "There are many ways to be a teacher" to me a few years before, invited me to a Bible study that he was hosting at his home. I had not been in contact with him since he left my community. He was retired now, but gathered a few people once a week to discuss the Bible. I informed him that I would attend the next session. He gave me directions on how to get to his house from the University of Illinois campus and I wrote them down. This event happened years before GPS existed.

On that day, the day I found my destination, I was traveling to somewhere I had never been before. I had never been to that part of town before, but I was confident that I would find my destination. As I was driving, I forgot the name of the street that I was supposed to turn on and made a wrong turn. After a block or two, I realized my mistake. I recalculated my route in my head. I could turn around and get back on the planned road, or I could drive south until I ran into the road that the pastor's house was on. I decided to just drive down that road until I found his house. The latter seemed the most convenient action to take.

I thank God that I decided to follow the path of the "wrong turn." That very wrong turn drove me right past the Greek Orthodox Church in Champaign, Illinois. I would have never found Christ's Church otherwise. I would have never found the Orthodox faith or known that it even existed still on earth. My prayers were answered that day because of that "wrong turn." That wrong turn to the left was really God's right turn for my life on that day.

As I drove past the church, its unique shape, its dome, and its cross on top caused me to stop my car and write down its name. My own efforts had led me to an impasse; I did not know where to go. God's intervention that day brought new information into consideration. Once I returned home, I immediately started investigating the Orthodox Church. I began finding materials and reading about the Orthodox Church: what the Orthodox Church was, what it believed, where it was from, what its goals and purpose were in this world. I found everything that I was looking for; I realized that this might be the Church.

It took me a little while to complete that journey which had begun a few months before on the day when I made that "wrong turn." After I had graduated from the University of Illinois and had come to the realization about what I had found that day, I finally attended the Orthodox Christian Church for the first time.

I had never been into such a building before. I had no idea what to expect; I was just sure that the Orthodox Christian Church believed the same things that were taught by the apostles. I wanted to see how they practiced ancient Christian beliefs. The smells, the sounds, and the sights were all startling. I listened to the words of the Divine Liturgy and was shocked. The faith was not something for text books. Even in the Liturgy, the work of the people, the faith was being taught to those present as they worshiped the One who had made it all possible. The priest taught and served the people of God while conducting the Divine Liturgy. The service of the Church was not to entertain; it was not a show. The Divine Liturgy was a means to guide the faithful into a deeper connection with Christ and His Church. The faith of the apostles was everywhere; I felt like I was in heaven.

Only later did I realize that I was not the first person to experience these feelings upon entering an Orthodox church for the first time. A thousand years before, travelers to Constantinople found themselves in a similar dilemma as I had in my own life. They traveled to their first liturgy but did not know whether they had traveled to heaven or if they still remained on earth. They simply knew that God lived in that place. I knew that I too had found God alive in the Orthodox Christian Church: He was worshiped, His faith was taught, and He was providing for the needs of His people through the Divine Liturgy within the Orthodox Church. I have never stopped attending the Divine Liturgy since that Sunday. I knew then that my calling was realized. God had called me to that place, and I was never going to leave. I was going to fulfill my ministry, and eventually my priesthood, as a member of the Orthodox Church.

The calling that I received from God was not a single, one-time event for me. I have described my calling as a series of three days, but these three days were also a part of a time that contained unique events in my life which left their mark on that entire period of my life. My calling was a process, a process that ultimately involved me growing closer to Christ and finding His Church, all at the same time. It involved multiple steps. As I advanced through each step, my efforts felt blessed, I was at peace, and I knew that God was on this journey with me. God was my pastor, gathering me into His people. He was offering me the opportunities to use the talents that He had provided for me in ways that were so much more fulfilling and joyful than I could have ever imagined.

I have modeled the pastoral care that I offer through my own priesthood after the way I was called both into ministry and into the Orthodox Church. Within my own priesthood, I have strived to be a pastor to those I have been charged to serve. The pastor that initially spoke to me never even mentioned to me the idea of becoming a minister, a priest. He simply offered me a thought and an opportunity for me to examine different perspectives. He may not have even known what he was doing at the time, but God did, and that pastor cooperated with God and fulfilled his ministry to me. I feel called to do the same.

The priest is there to be a means of connection between the people and God. The priest is a person to be trusted for advice, when all the roads forward seem blocked. The priest is there to love us, to support us, to bring the divine perspective of the Church into consideration in how we live our lives. The priest is there to see beyond our own self-imposed blinders or preconceived notions of ourselves, our lives, and what will allow us to find joy. The priest is there, ultimately to teach, to assist, and to walk with us as we consider how to live our lives in new and divine ways, utilizing those God-given gifts and opportunities bestowed upon us from on high.

On these three specific days out of my life, God called me into a new and deeper relationship with Him and His Church. Those days started out normal and were going according to plan until each day took a "wrong turn" and proceeded on a different path. These divine interventions in my life took me to the place where I needed to be, where I wanted to be, where I had hoped to be, even though I was simply trying to live my life for the benefit of others. I have never felt I was the same person since.

Father Nichalas March serves at
Holy Transfiguration Church in Mason City, Iowa.

Father Christos Mihalopoulos

The understanding of the terms "service" and "dedication" were truly foreign to me. As a young boy growing up in the southwestern suburbs of Chicago, I was encased in a bubble of a life: a middle class family, father, mother, older sister, and older brother. We learned to work hard, study, and grow to be something in life. My journey was similar to the journeys that millions of people have. Yet seeing the struggles my parents had as immigrants, and I myself being a first- generation Greek-American, I had questions about what was the purpose of life, and how could I live a meaningful life? In answering these questions, I came to the conclusion that we must be driven, and we must be goal-oriented toward something that makes this world a better place.

The only way I was able to recognize that challenge was the development of my faith and foundations. I am "cradle Orthodox," meaning that I was born and raised in a Greek Orthodox Christian household. I was in church on a regular basis. By the age of three, I was already in the holy altar to serve as a young altar boy. The robes were too big, and they had a small black one for me. I was quoted as saying, "I don't like this black one. I want the one the priest has on!" I guess even from there my story began evolving, and I was preparing myself for my future calling.

My father, Panayiotis Mihalopoulos, was a simple man from Tripoli, Greece. He came to Chicago in 1971 when he was twenty-one, after he married my mother, Nikki, nee Digenis (Digenopoulos), who was only nineteen then. They came to Chicago to work at various family restaurants and to begin a life with my maternal grandparents. They struggled in the early years, just as every young couple does. They also had my sister and brother very early on in their marriage. By 1980, my father was growing tired of the restaurant life. They moved to the southern suburbs of Chicago, to Burbank, and they began attending Holy Cross Church in Justice, IL. There my father had a restaurant called "Thames," and he met many clergy from the South Side, as it was called: Fr. Byron Papanikolaou, Fr. Jon Magoulias, Fr. Gabriel Karambis, Fr. Constantine Bithos, Fr. Anargyros Stavropoulos, and others. All of these served the South Side parishes of the Diocese of Chicago. Each clergyman had an impact on my father as he found his way from a simple Greek-American restauranteur to a future iconographer, chanter, and dedicated follower of the Lord.

My family's epiphany truly is the foundation to my future calling, because I was born in 1987, and by then my parents had become active participants in the Greek Orthodox Church. My father was beginning his calling to become an iconographer through much trial and error. As I was growing up, I was surrounded by church leaders and role models constantly. My father was slowly beginning to receive orders for icons from clergy who were taking a chance on this inexperienced and self-taught iconographer, who was working at Maryann/S. Rosen's Bakery as a delivery driver. Father Gabriel Karambis, at St. Nicholas Church in Oak Lawn, gave my father his first paid order of two icons that would go with the crucifixion of our Lord. This was a wonderful example of a clergyman taking a chance on my father. Whenever any priest placed an order from my father, we as a family would attend services there.

That is why I grew up with so many examples of service and dedication, because I traveled with my father constantly and met all these examples of Christian love and stewardship. The story continued with St. Spyridon in Palos Heights and Fr. Anargyros Stavropoulos, who was a friend of my father's from their days growing up in Tripoli, Greece. This is where I called home, as I attended church there often; I went to Plutarchos Greek School there, I was an altar boy, played GOAL basketball, and participated in GOYA.

My father always had a soft spot for smaller churches, so after St. Spyridon, we were helping and supporting the community of the Assumption of the Theotokos in Hegewisch, Il, with Fr. George Phillipas as their priest. What a wonderful human being who encouraged me, supported me, and was a true example of Christ's enduring love for His people! The community was not a cathedral; it wasn't large, it wasn't filled with grandeur, but it had a sweetness that as a young man I couldn't comprehend. Now as an adult I cherish the memory, because it truly is at its core a community of love and service to God. My father was commissioned to draw a few icons for St. Spyridon in Palos Heights, and then he was commissioned to paint icons at All Saints Church in Joliet. There, Fr. Stephen Bithos became a great friend to our family and a wonderful mentor to me.

Father Bithos worked tirelessly with my father as he painted most of All Saints with Byzantine iconography; Fr. Stephen continued to be an example of true service to God's people. As my father was doing work at All Saints, he also began work at Assumption Church in Olympia Fields (now in Homer Glen). This is where I met Fr. Sotirios (Sam) Dimitriou, another inspiring clergyman who also guided me throughout my teenager years.

The assignment of Fr. Tilemahos Alikakos to St. Spyridon in Palos Heights was the catalyst for my renewed optimism to follow him into the priesthood, because of his love of the faith, his understanding of liturgical and chanting practices, and his realistic approach; he was in his late thirties when he was assigned to St. Spyridon. He understood us high schoolers, he made GOYA fun, he was encouraging in the holy altar, and he led me in studying Byzantine music at the psaltirion (chanter's stand), so that one day I too could help lead services at the chanter stand.

After I decided to go to the University of Illinois at Chicago, near Greektown in Chicago, I was given a great opportunity to see true service and dedication in the form of my future spiritual father, Fr. Chris P. Kerhulas, who was serving St. Basil's Church in Chicago. I attended St. Basil's one Sunday in September of 2005, which was my first in college. At the end of the service when I went to receive antidoron, Fr. Chris spoke to me to ask who I was. He remembered my father, and our connection was immediate. He encouraged me to come to church as often as possible while I was on campus. He encouraged me to begin chanting at the chanter's stand with his chanters. He allowed me to help in the holy altar. He took me at my best, and definitely took me at my worst. He was dynamic and vibrant, and he was different from any other clergyman I met. His differences allowed me to recognize how I too could embrace a life of joy in service and dedication to others.

I was assigned to become the head chanter at All Saints Church in Joliet in 2006, and I remained as the head chanter until I decided to enter the Holy Cross Greek Orthodox School of Theology seminarian program the Fall of 2010. At the School of Theology, many more clergy from the school and surrounding Boston Metropolis gave me more fuel and ambition to realize that the life I was entering, dedicated to our Lord and His people, is the most rewarding life of all.

An aspect of my life that contributed to my calling to serve might sound weird when I express it. The food service industry was also a great jumping off point into my future ministry. I worked as a busboy and host at a Bennigan's in Oak Brook when I was seventeen. I still worked as a host/ server when I went to UIC in Chicago at the Bennigan's in downtown Chicago on Michigan avenue for five years. I concluded my work at Bennigan's and began working at a fine dining restaurant called Carmichael's Steakhouse in the West Loop of downtown Chicago, where I stayed for five years. Even when I was at the School of Theology, I worked during my three years of studies at Legal Seafoods in Chestnut Hill, Massachusetts. Every restaurant I worked at taught me the greatest life lessons. Everyone is different, and everyone is unique. I learned from the people I served, their families, their professions, and their lifestyles. The restaurants afforded me the opportunity to see the entire world, the "real world," so that when I went out to serve and love all of God's people, I had experiences that humbled me to recognize the uniqueness of everyone.

The last support to my future office of the holy priesthood was finding my beloved wife, Presvytera Toni Poteres, and her family, who supported my future service. Toni comes from a family dedicated to the Church. My father-in-law is a Greek Orthodox priest, Fr. Theodore Poteres of Saints Constantine and Helen Greek Orthodox Cathedral in

Merrillville, IN, who served with his incredible wife, the late Presvytera Tulla Poteres. They are two incredible people who raised two wonderful children and dedicated their entire lives serving God, glorifying His holy name, and bringing people closer to God by recognizing the unconditional love and mercy He has for all of us.

There are so many people who helped me to understand the "Calling to Serve." In reality, it was in the simplest of ways that I came to understand what the meaning of life is for me. The goal is to live life fully, in a Christ-like manner, and to make an impact in the world, one person at a time. My predecessors, my mentors, my spiritual fathers, my role models, my examples—all of them are the reason why I decided to go into the holy priesthood. It's also thanks to my hierarchs who instilled their trust in me to serve the people of God: the late Metropolitan Iakovos of Chicago, His Eminence Metropolitan Nathanael of Chicago, and His Grace Bishop Timothy of Hexamilion, our chancellor. Their support and continued guidance have encouraged me and challenged me to do more to serve all of God's people.

God works with the grace of the Holy Spirit to guide those to follow in His footsteps to a much greater calling. In recognizing our own humility and taking a deep breath to listen to God's will, even though it might not be verbal or right in front of us, we are afforded the opportunity to recognize a more complete life—a life dedicated to Christ and His people.

Every person, male or female, is called to serve. To serve someone is the greatest gift and the humblest expression anyone can offer. In this extreme humility, we recognize God. We comprehend God. We know God. We are one with God. We love God. We all have the opportunity to grow in a life with Christ when we understand we need to grow with each other. We should break down barriers, demolish political ideologies, and ignore divisions, so that we can allow the love that God has given us to be the glue that connects us to our fellow man.

Once we have accomplished this, we will be able to find countless ways to embrace a life "called to serve" and will, with proper adoration, glorify His holy name and receive the gift to come unto the ages of ages. Amen!

Father Christos Mihalopoulos serves
at Saint Nectarios Church in Palatine, Illinois.

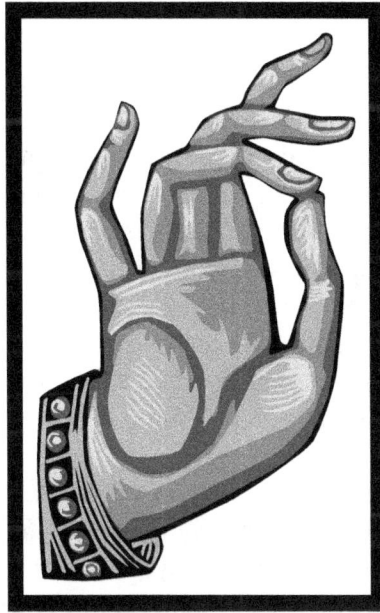

Father Doug Papulis

My calling was not a Damascus experience. My calling was rooted and nurtured in the Orthodox Christian faith, lived and loved in the home by my parents and maternal grandparents (my paternal grandparents had died before I was born). My grandparents lived with us throughout my life—my grandfather, Socrates, and I even shared a bedroom, as did my sister with our grandmother, Angeliki. Daily, I witnessed their love for Christ and His Church. They chanted from their Synekdismos books the hymns of the various church services. Their chanting filled our home. When they chanted, there was no radio, television, or stereo music turned on (no "danga dounga," as my grandmother would say).

Every day they prayed in the morning, in the evening, and before meals. Every day they read the Scriptures. I am blessed and thankful to have their well-used Synekdismos books and Bibles; and I still have the Holy Week Book (edited by Fr. George Papadeas of blessed memory) which my grandparents gave me in 1973. Now tattered and with pages falling out from many decades of use, I still use it if only for one service, the Bridegroom Service on Palm Sunday evening, in honor and remembrance of my grandparents, who nurtured my love for God and the Church. Like my grandparents, the patriarch and matriarch of the family, my parents also read the Scriptures and prayed. I remember my grandmother, with her censer in hand, walking room to room at 7:00 a.m. every Saturday morning to bless us and the icons. Each member of the family had to be up, dressed, teeth brushed, face and hands washed, and standing by his or her bed as my grandmother approached and made the sign of the cross with the incense billowing from her hand-held censer before us, our icons, and all the rooms in the house—and, of course, there was no music, no "danga dounga," only the chanting of church hymns.

I recall one Saturday morning in particular, when, having been blessed by my grandmother shortly after 7:00 am, I began to phone one of my friends to come over to play. I was about eight years old. My mother saw me dialing, and she, with great surprise and concern, asked what I was doing – whom was I calling so early on a Saturday morning? When I told her, she ordered me to hang up and informed me that I couldn't call friends so early on a Saturday morning because they (like everyone else in the neighborhood) was fast asleep. I responded that we were awake, to which my mom chuckled and said, "Yes, dear, that's because we're Orthodox Christians, and it's not proper to be in bed when your grandmother comes around with the censer to bless us and the house." I just assumed that everyone had their homes blessed on Saturday mornings! Like chanting, praying, reading the Bible, censing the home, fasting was routine, a natural part of our family's life. Helping others, being generous and kind towards others was not an occasional or seasonal act, but a constant mindset and action. My parents and grandparents loved God and they loved their neighbor. Their spiritual discipline and piety, their love of God and of the Orthodox Faith infused our home and became my love of God and the Orthodox faith. Holy Tradition was lived and carefully and lovingly handed down from one generation (my grandparents) to another generation (my parents) and to another (my siblings and me). God and Orthodoxy were not esoteric or cerebral exercises, nor were they remote and occasional presences. Christ and our faith were tangible, everyday realities which permeated our life. Our Lord and faith informed who we were. Indeed, when a question was asked, the answer given by my elders (parents and grandparents) was always framed in light of Orthodox Christianity. Never did I hear my grandmother say, for example, that she thought or believed a certain way; rather, she would answer our questions with a question, "What does the Bible say?" or "What do the saints say?" or "What does the Church say?" or "What does God say?" Sometimes she would ask all these questions together, indicating that they meant the same thing, that the answer lies not in one's opinion, but in the truth of our Orthodox Christian Tradition and mindset or phronema. I learned in the home to live and love and serve God and our Orthodox Church. My parents and grandparents were the primary source and foundation of my call to serve.

What I witnessed at home in my family was reinforced by what I saw in our beloved parish priest, Fr. George Tsoukalas, who loved serving both God and the parishioners of the Annunciation Greek Orthodox Church in Woburn, Massachusetts. Father George was a serious shepherd. He was serious, because he cared about the well-being of his flock; he cared about the life and the salvation of his parishioners. Father George Tsoukalas lived and breathed Orthodoxy. With much energy and enthusiasm, he taught the faith by his words, actions, and demeanor, and he did all this and everything with much joy and love. He showed that genuine, eternal love is based on the sure foundation of the Triune God. This made an important impression on me, a teenager, during the decade of the 70s, when one's opinion was idolized, and love was based on whatever anyone believed or wanted it to be. Father George taught and showed that, on the contrary, love is not subjective, based on one's opinion or whims, but is grounded in the reality of a merciful, forgiving, and compassionate God, who is present in every moment of our lives. Father George exuded Christ-like love, and he embraced everyone with it. Father Tsoukalas literally gripped you with his zeal and love for Christ and His people! What I saw in Fr. George confirmed and strengthened what I saw and lived at home, that God and His Church and the Orthodox faith are truly essential for a full and blessed life.

My grandparents died before I was ordained, but I had told them when I was a junior in high school that I was thinking about the holy priesthood to serve God and the Church. My grandparents and parents all received the news with much joy and gave me their blessings and encouragement. I will never forget my grandfather weeping with joy and humility that one of his grandsons would one day be a priest. Father George Tsoukalas took me under his wing and mentored me. In addition to assisting with cleaning the church, altar items, and the landscaping around the church building that I had done previously, he now had me by his side during church services, as well as visiting parishioners with him in their homes, in the hospitals, and in the nursing homes. He offered me instruction, guidance, and advice, which to this day are a great help. I would not be the person or priest I am if it were not for these remarkable people. Their dedication, their Christ-like example, their service to our Lord and God and Savior Jesus Christ and His Church led and called me to serve as a priest.

Father Doug Papulis serves
at Saint Nicholas Church in St. Louis, Missouri.

Father Theofanis Rauch

The story of my calling to serve God as a priest isn't the story of one extraordinary moment where I clearly heard God calling me. The calling I experienced wasn't tied to one great miracle, or one life-changing experience. Rather, my calling to serve God is a story of both a small "mustard seed" (Lk. 13) and a "still small voice" (1 Kings 19:12) that were placed in my heart from my earliest childhood. The most honest and direct way I can describe what this calling feels like is a companion that has journeyed through life with me. This calling has never felt as if it came from me, or that I decided on it. I have never fully understood it. From the beginning, my calling has felt like it was given to me, and I have lived my life with this companion in my heart every step of the way.

As a young child, when I initially recognized this calling in my heart, the first people I shared this part of my soul with were my parents, Theofanis and Vasilike Rauch. God blessed me with such faithful, loving, tender-hearted, and empathetic parents. Looking back, I am amazed by their faith. For many people, a toddler speaking about feeling called to serve God as a priest would be written off as just something cute. However, my parents, in their sincere faith, treated the presence of God, even in the heart of a young child, with great reverence. They nurtured this small seed through their love, their patience in answering the difficult questions I had, their compassion when I would wake up in the middle of the night feeling overwhelmed by the great responsibility of this calling, and through the example of their own relationships with Christ.

As I grew a little older, the next relationship that watered the seed of this calling in my heart was my spiritual father, Fr. Constantine Aliferakis. Father Constantine was the priest at my home parish, and it was he who gave my desire to serve Christ even more depth and meaning. It's hard to write down just how much Fr. Constantine taught me. He showed me how beautiful the Divine Liturgy is, as are all the services of the church. He showed me that our life in Christ is deepened and strengthened through having living relationships with the Panagia and all of the Saints. He often told me, "The priesthood is a Golgotha. You will face a great cross, but at the foot of the cross is where the most beautiful flowers bloom." This saying is one that I saw confirmed through his own life and witness and am now experiencing in my own life.

One more relationship from my childhood that further strengthened and formed my calling was my relationship with my great-grandmother, Vasilike Kostouros. My great-grandmother faced many hardships in her life. From being in a war-stricken part of Greece, to caring for the orphan children in her village even though she didn't have enough means to care for herself, to facing the death of her child at a young age, my great-grandmother had every opportunity to have a hardened heart and a pessimistic outlook on life. However, my great-grandmother was a saintly woman of peace, joy, and gratitude to God. Of all of the lessons she imparted to me, one stands above the rest and has shaped the course of my understanding of the priesthood. She would always tell me, "Theofani, life is hard. But if you can be a source of comfort to someone, even for just a moment, you have done something beautiful." This saying is the guiding motto for my life of service, and I found my great-grandmother's advice fulfilled in the words of St. Paul, "Bear one another's burdens, and so fulfill the law of Christ" (Gal. 6:2).

When the time came for me to head off to college, I left for Boston to attend Hellenic College and Holy Cross Greek Orthodox School of Theology in Brookline, Massachusetts. I spent six years there, and in that time I underwent many life-changing experiences. The first of these experiences was my time in prison ministry under the guidance of Fr. Antony Hughes. What started as a way to earn service hours for a field education class ended up being the most transformative experience of my academic career. I remember first walking through the heavy doors of the prison and the sinking feeling of fear as they locked behind me. I remember walking into a room filled with inmates and thinking I was somehow going to help them or teach them something. But the truth is, what I experienced was that the Holy Spirit was alive and active in the walls of that prison.

Several of the inmates and I became good friends. They told me stories of how their lives of violence and crime all changed when they received a Bible and started attending Fr. Antony's classes on a weekly basis. One inmate told me how he was the most problematic inmate in the entire prison. He often had to be sedated because he would not stop fighting with inmates and guards alike every single day. However, after encountering Christ in the Gospel, he changed his way of life, and became one of the gentlest souls I have ever encountered. He went from being the most violent and aggressive inmate to being the first person to successfully start a garden within the prison walls. I saw so tangibly how the Holy Spirit is able to completely transform the hearts of those who are humble. This experience showed me that "with God all things are possible" (Mt. 19:26).

The second experience that completely shaped my identity and calling to serve God was meeting my wife, Presvytera Lydia, and starting our family with our two beautiful children, Fanourios and Theodore. Presvytera Lydia and I met when she came to visit the seminary to see her sister and her nieces. By God's grace, and through the intercessions of St. Fanourios, we both found each other there and immediately fell in love. We were married two years later, and in the next few years we were blessed with our two sons.

Presvytera Lydia has become my greatest companion, friend, partner, and inspiration in this life. Her example of simple and powerful faith, meekness, and true selflessness continually motivates and shapes the way that I strive to love and serve others as a priest. My family has been my greatest blessing because it has revealed to me that truly loving someone goes far deeper than I previously thought possible. True love and true joy, much like the other greatest blessings in life, all require great sacrifice. Experiencing the love that comes with being a husband and a father has been a powerful teacher in how to love others, and the support and strength of my wife and children makes it possible for me to face the difficulties that come with my calling.

There is one more part of my journey of discerning my calling which really cemented my conviction to serve our Lord and to help bear the burdens of others. This encounter happened a few months before I was ordained. After I graduated from seminary, I was living in Indiana with Presvytera Lydia and our first son, Fanourios. I had submitted my paperwork for ordination at this time, and I was anxiously waiting to hear back from the Archdiocese.

Suddenly, we were hit with some devastating news. I remember I was outside when Presvytera ran out to me and said, "I'm so sorry," with tears in her eyes. I asked what's wrong, and she replied, "She's gone. I'm so sorry." I looked at Presvytera's phone and my heart sank as I received the news that one of my dearest friends had passed away from a drug overdose. We had been friends since high school, and I knew she struggled with addiction since that time. Throughout our friendship, we always tried our best to support each other, and I did my best to be there for her and love her as she bravely fought against her addiction. At this point, I thought she had been clean for the past year. I was so heartbroken, and in a way, I felt like I had failed her, because I wasn't there for her in her most difficult moment. What made it even worse was that Presvytera and I were supposed to meet her two days later at the park for Fanourios and her son to have a playdate.

We arrived at the day of the funeral, and it was a heart-wrenching day to say the least. I saw friends I hadn't seen for years all gathered together to pray for our friend and comfort her family. What stung the most was when my friend's dad approached me in tears and said, "You're going to be a priest, right? Then tell me why God would take my daughter from me. You're supposed to be able to help me, right? Please just help me to hurt less." I remember being completely frozen. I didn't know what I could possibly say in that moment. All I could do was give him a hug and muster a weak, "I'm so sorry," as I was overcome with tears as well. It was in this moment that I felt my final push to serve our

Lord as a priest. I felt so weak and helpless in this moment. I felt as if I couldn't help my friend's dad at all even though it was my life's motto to "bear one another's burdens." Even though I felt helpless and afraid, at the same time I felt hope and comfort in our Lord. I knew I couldn't do much to help others on my own, but with our Lord all things are possible. I vowed to devote my life to serve our Lord and to bear the burdens of His people through His grace, love, light, peace, and hope. This moment will always have an impact on living out my calling to serve Christ.

Reflecting on my path to serving God as His priest, I am overwhelmed by how much of my journey I owe to the beautiful relationships I have experienced in my life. The calling to serve God as a clergyman, or to serve God in any way, can be confusing and difficult to discern. I believe I would have had much more difficulty discerning this calling and following the path God has called me to if it wasn't for the many beautiful people around me teaching me through the example of their own lives, nurturing this calling, and fanning the flames of desire to serve our Lord in my heart. This is the beautiful part of living a life in Christ. As St. Paul says, "There are diversities of gifts, but the same Spirit. There are differences of ministries, but the same Lord. And there are diversities of activities, but it is the same God who works all in all" (1 Cor. 12:4-6). We are all called to serve our Lord in different ways, but we are all united, and this is what makes the Body of Christ so vibrant in the world. We are never alone when we serve our Lord.

From all of the examples I mentioned above, to my grandparents, friends, koumbaroi, brother clergy, the Panagia, St. Fanourios, St. Porphyrios, and all of the saints, I am grateful to God that He gave me the gift of those around me. A wise priest, Fr. Constantine Eliades, described the blessing of relationships best when he told me, "The people God puts in your life are a gift. Each relationship is like a beautiful star. It's good to take a step back sometimes and just admire the beautiful constellation that God has arranged in your sky."

If I can offer a small piece of advice in helping to discern one's calling to serve God in life, it is to look for Christ everywhere, especially in relationships. First and foremost, cultivating a living relationship with Christ is essential. Pray to Him and speak to Him from your own heart. Be honest with Him and with yourself, and He will always help you and guide you to what is good. Look for Christ in all of your other relationships as well. Whether it is your families, friends, fellow parishioners, coworkers, or even someone you bump into on the street, God puts people in our lives for a reason. Our relationships can become our greatest treasure and make the rest of our lives so beautiful. Look for Christ in the hearts of others, and in this way, we will find a taste of paradise even in this life. As St. Apollo once said, "If I have seen my brother, I have seen Christ" (Sayings of the Desert Fathers).

Father Theofanis Rauch serves
at All Saints Church in Peoria, Illinois.

Father Peter Sarolas

When I was about the age of twelve, I really did not know much about what it meant to be a Greek Orthodox Christian. My parish priest is responsible for opening my eyes to being a Greek Orthodox Christian. He would take us (the handful of youth in his parish) to lock-ins and retreats, and we would learn about our faith in different ways. I remember attending Camp Fanari and going to confession for the very first time.

Confession was something that was not talked about at home, but going to confession as a twelve-year-old was a big thing. In fact, it is something that I continue to do today.

In 1984, I remember my parents making the decision, through the encouragement of my parish priest, to go to Ionian Village. I remember meeting several Greek Orthodox Christians who were the same age as me or a couple years older than me.

There are two excursions that stick out in my mind. One was the trip to Zakythnos and the other was to Aegina. I remember seeing a young boy; he must have been five or so, and he was dressed in a black robe. I asked one of the counselors why he was dressed like that. The answer was the parents could not conceive a child and they prayed to St. Dionysios and their prayer was answered. I remember venerating the relics. It was my very first time seeing a "walking saint"whose body is intact.

The other experience was visiting the Island of Aegina and seeing the relics of St. Nectarios. I remember that hearing about this modern-day saint and the miracles that were attributed to him was really an experience. I also remember putting my ear on the tomb of St. Nektarios like the other campers, counselors, and priests. I remember tears running down my face and others around me hearing the sound from the tomb of St. Nectarios. Learning about both St.Dionysios and St. Nectaris during Ionian Village was a life changing event for me.

My parish priest was responsible for these experiences, and for that I am grateful. Throughout my high school years, we would talk about faith and that helped shape my calling to the Holy Priesthood. While at Hellenic College and Holy Cross School of Theology my parish priest was a constant voice in my life. He would check in with me an send little care packages, etc. When I graduated from the seminary, he was a constant in my life. Fast forward to today, he is that presence and influence in my life and there are no words to define what he means to me and who I am today.

Father Peter Sarolas serves
at Saint George Church in Chicago, Illinois.

Father Dimitri Tobias

W	*e love because He first loved us — 1 Jn. 4:19*
		The word "calling" implies the passive nature of the
		recipient. There is no active agency outside of the response
to the call. Therefore, no glory or ownership of the call can be grasped
by the recipient. "I am the vine, you are the branches. He who abides
in Me, and I in him, bears much fruit; for without Me you can do
nothing" (Matt. 15:5).

For my story, the call to serve the holy flock of Christ did not result
from my own actions, but those of my parents. My parents desired
to have children immediately after they were married, but they were
unable to conceive. For six years they struggled, and no therapies or
interventions worked for them. They tried to adopt, but in the 1970s,
adoption agencies considered military families less than ideal for
children. Both of my parents served in the United States Air Force and
would move bases every few years, so they persisted and waited.

Now, one might think the parents of a future clergyman would be devout, but that was not the case. My mother, a first generation Greek-American, felt pride in her faith as an Orthodox Christian, but not in a good way. While understanding nothing about the faith, she only knew "Orthodox is right and everyone else is wrong." Orthodoxy is the only true religion. This arrogant and "othering" belief structure does not foster love, but this can hardly be seen as her fault.

My mother grew up in a stifling home, in which her parents picked every aspect of her life. When they insisted she marry a man she did not love, she joined the United States Air Force to escape. This spark of independence caused her parents to disown her. The consistent and painful hatred of her mother beat my mother to a place where she needed to believe in something as absolute. Unfortunately, her religious education did not provide anything beyond the belief that Orthodoxy was supreme.

My father, divorced, met my mother in England where they were both stationed at the time and fell in love. When they married, my mother told him that he did not have to convert to Orthodoxy, but that they would only attend one church and it would be the Greek church. My father is the product of many nationalities, primarily Scottish and German, and while he was raised as a Presbyterian, he did not have a solid belief structure or firm allegiance to his church, so he acquiesced to her only demand on their marriage.

Not long after, perhaps three years into their marriage, he and my mother attended a couples' lock-in retreat at the Orthodox church in Omaha, Nebraska, where they were stationed after their assignment in England concluded. The passion in which the retreat leader, an archimandrite, explained the faith, spoke to my father's heart and by the time the sun rose, he declared with tears in his eyes that he would join the Orthodox Church.

Despite their newfound joy in the faith, my parents were plagued by the agony of childlessness. Despairing every time they would hear of a child abused or abandoned on the news, my parents lamented that while they desperately wanted children to love, individuals would harm children or treat them like an inconvenience to be abandoned.

Adding to this misery, my mother had to deal with the hatred of her mother, who did not approve of my mother marrying a xeno. My father could not believe any mother would actually hate their own daughter and would try to comfort her, saying this must be a misunderstanding. This changed when he witnessed her sobbing on the phone one evening. He picked up the other line in another room to listen and could not believe the vitriol spewing from the woman's lips to wound her only child. He yelled into the phone, "I would not even speak to a dog the way you speak to your daughter! How dare you!" as he slammed the phone into the drywall, leaving a fist-sized hole. Panting in pain for his wife, he cried that he had no idea their relationship was so bad.

Nevertheless, my mother never gave up hope and continuously tried to win her mother's affection. Like a knife to the gut, she would tell my mother that God had cursed her, and she should just accept that she is unfit to be a mother. "Don't you get it?! God is trying to tell you something because you can't conceive!"

Wondering if this could be true, and full of pain from six long years, my parents sat down with their priest and asked what they should do. They shared everything with him, and he replied after prayerful consideration, "Have you ever prayed to the Theotokos for help?" Because their faith was still in its infancy, they admitted that they had never considered praying to the Panagia.

My mother went home that night and prayed in front of her icon and said, "Mother of God, please, I know I may not be the best candidate to be a mom, but I want a baby. Please, please let me have a baby to love, to hold, to embrace. I promise I will do right by the child. I promise I won't waste the gift of a child, and I promise you I will give my child to you and to your Son if you will please, please give me a child."

Nine months later, my older brother was born and thirteen months after that, I was born. Three years later my younger brother was born. The Theotokos immediately answered her prayer. My mother did everything in her power to live up to her promise. She showered her three sons with love and dutifully brought us to church every week.

From the age of five I never wavered in stating that when I grew up I would be a priest. I never understood where this self-assurance came from, but when I heard this story realized my calling came as a response to my mother's promise.

While my parents never mentioned this story to me while growing up, they shared it with me when I declared I wanted to go to seminary.

They told me they had quietly known this call to become a priest came from the Mother of God. Despite this, they never pushed me or influenced me in that direction. They adamantly wanted their children to choose their own path in life.

They shared a few examples with me that they told me were hints:

When I was a toddler, during the Divine Liturgy in which the priest said loudly, "Blessed is He who comes in the name of the Lord," I jumped down from my father's lap and ran up the center aisle to the holy altar. I reached the solea before my father was able to grab me and return to his pew with an embarrassed smile. My mother stated that she felt in her soul at that moment that her promise to the Theotokos was going to be fulfilled through her middle son.

A second story took place when I was five or six. Because my parents were again stationed in England, they took advantage of the proximity to go to Italy. While there, they brought us to a Roman Catholic monastery. While they were engrossed with the tour, they suddenly realized I was nowhere to be found. In a panic, they held onto the other two boys and frantically looked around the ancient building until they saw a friar running with a look of frustration. Instinctively, they knew it was their child causing that annoyance and so they ran after him. All at once, the friar skidded to a halt and his mouth hung agape as he looked through a doorway that had stanchions in place to indicate it was off limits to the tourists. My parents came up behind him and looked inside the room, which they saw was a small chapel. There, in front of the altar, stood their son repeatedly doing his cross and singing, Agios o Theos (Holy God).

The friar turned to my parents and asked them in broken English if this child was their son. They nodded, embarrassment evident on their faces for the fact of their trespassing child. He then asked them, "Praying?" Again, they nodded, and my father said, "I will get him. I am so sorry!" The friar held up his hand and said with admiration in his voice, "No. Let him finish." As soon as I finished chanting the hymn they escorted me out of the chapel and again apologized to the friar.

Growing up, moving from base to base was hard for me. Making new friends never came easy. The only constant that grounded me was the holy altar. Serving in the altar each week made me feel safe, loved and I knew I belonged.

Children can be cruel to the new kid, especially in middle school. I had gum mashed in my hair, paper balls thrown in my face, my cross ripped from my throat and thrown on the ground. I did not share these instances with my parents, because I didn't want to worry them. Instead, I wrote a letter to God asking for His help. While the instances of being called "Hair Boy" or "Jew Boy" because of my curly hair did not diminish, I began to feel ever more at peace in the altar. I began to learn how to pray in earnest with my prayer corner, to pray for my enemies and to deepen my love for God. This brought me peace.

One of the consistent elements I found in my studies of Orthodox spirituality was the healing power of tears. Yet, despite my hours of prayers and my desire to serve, I could not cry for my sins or myself. I brought this to my spiritual fathers' attention throughout the years before seminary and during seminary. I felt like a fraud.

Then, I was instructed by a priest to add the Supplicatory Canon to the Sweetest Lord Jesus into the Small Compline service. This canon utilizes the name of Jesus, which saves, to bring to mind His love and His protection. However, when I read the Doxastikon of the Seventh Ode I trembled:

O Christ Jesus, ten thousand times have I, the hapless one, promised You repentance, O my Jesus, but, wretch that I am, I lied to You. Therefore, I cry to You, my Jesus: Enlighten my soul which yet remains unfeeling, O Christ, the God of our Fathers.

This prayer spoke to the nature of my unfeeling heart and my unworthiness as His child. I broke down into hapless sobs. Finally, finally I could cry for my sins. Finally, I experienced those blessed cleansing tears, and I felt my very being transformed as a result.

A second instance of this answer to my prayers from my Lord and Savior occurred after I had graduated seminary. My friends and classmates had all either married or been ordained. I felt adrift, alone and hopeless. I was driving in the city of Chicago and screamed in my car, "Do You even care? I left everything for You and I am so alone. Why am I here?"

In frustration, and embarrassed that I cried out to Christ my God like a petulant child, I switched the radio on to lose myself in some music. I was not prepared to hear the first words that cried out of the speakers, "I LOVE YOU!"

Hanging my head in shame, I sobbed like a baby. My God loves me and always has. He will never abandon me.

Soon after, I took the job of a pastoral lay assistant. Because my job was primarily to minister to children and young families, I did not have the opportunity to meet girls. I was like a horse with blinders on his eyes, focusing only on the task at hand. Then, when my mother came to visit, she asked me why I had not met anyone yet despite serving such a large parish. I stupidly said there were no prospects. She said she would pray to the Theotokos for my future bride and lit candles for this mystery girl for years.

Meanwhile, a beautiful soul inside and out had decided she wanted to return to God and church because her job kept her away on Sundays, and she felt disconnected. She began to go to morning Bible studies to deepen her relationship. My mother met her briefly during a visit and enquired if she was single. When she pointed this girl out to me, I said that this beautiful woman would never want to be with a person like me. After some gentle prodding from my mother, I asked this incredible girl out and we began to date. Eventually, she and I would marry. This would never have happened without those prayers.

This incredible girl's family also had a close relationship with Mother of God. Their village church in Greece was dedicated to her and on many occasions, they had experienced direct interventions from the Mother of God to save them from harm physically and spiritually. The final clue that this joining of two souls to serve the flock of Christ through the intercessions of the Theotokos was my wife's name: Maria.

There isn't space to mention all the clergy and hierarchs who shaped my formation. The final story of this calling came shortly after I was married and while I was putting in my paperwork for ordination.

One of my GOYAn's suffered a horrific freak accident in high school while playing a now-banned game called "One Ball Dodge Ball." While he and another boy had moved to grab the singular dodge ball, the other boy accidentally kneed him on the side of the head. The injured boy convulsed and foamed at the mouth. When they brought the boy to the hospital, the extent of the traumatic brain injury was revealed, and the chances of survival appeared very slim.

Because of my love for the Theotokos, I immediately organized daily paraklesis services on the boy's behalf at the church I served. Every night, be it parents, the boy's friends, or people who wanted to pray for him, hymns rose to the Theotokos to intercede to her Son on behalf of the boy whose baptismal name was Mammas. As it happened, after one such service, a dear friend who himself is now a priest said to me, "I didn't know his name was Mammas. I only knew him as Michael. Last year, I served as a counselor at Ionian Village and was blessed to visit the Church of St. Mammas. I have an icon of the saint that was blessed over the sacred relics. Let's bring that icon to Michael's hospital bed tomorrow."

We traveled together and prayed to St. Mammas that the boy be saved.

A few days later, the boy's mother awoke, having fallen asleep praying over her son, to see him smiling at her and say, "Hi, Mom."

While there was fear that this injury might impact him permanently, these were laid to rest when he performed a magnificent piano performance that May at the GOYA talent show.

The significance of this miracle and its relevance to my calling is this: in August of that year I was informed that I would be ordained to the holy priesthood. The date the Metropolitan had chosen for this event: Sunday, September 2nd, the feast of St. Mammas.

I am grateful to God that he allowed His Mother to guide us to Him that we might be saved and to serve His holy people that they too may know His love. My mother, for her part, asked me to serve forty liturgies for her departed mother, who sadly never forgave her daughter. I am proud of my mother's love and faith which did not show bitterness towards her but forgave this unnatural hatred by following the example of our mother, the Panagia.

Father Dimitri Tobias serves at
Saint John the Baptist Church in Des Plaines, Illinois.

Father John Tsikalas

O *Lord, how sweet are thy words to my taste, sweeter than honey to my mouth! — Ps. 118:103*

More than any one reasoned argument or significant experience I've had in life, it's this verse from the Psalms that encapsulates the calling I received to serve Christ as a priest in His Church. How sweet are His words, indeed! The Church—her life, rhythm, teachings, and example— when applied diligently, surpass explanation and understanding. The Church's sweetness allows us to operate on a spiritual plane of being (St. Sophrony of Essex) and to thrive in this world as disciples of our Lord. Christianity has been and continues to be characterized with all sorts of pejoratives. Yet, for me, Christ's salvific commandments are best described as sweetness.

I will do my best in this brief reflection to explain the calling I received as a young man to pursue the holy priesthood. My calling is not one of God supernaturally intervening in a dream or apparition. There was no lightning moment. Rather, the steady and lived experience of growing up in the Orthodox Christian landscape of the United States facilitated my pursuit of ordained ministry. My calling is filled with individuals, many of whom are faithful priests, who selflessly transmitted their love for God into my life and eventually gave me no other option than to pursue ordination. As the Psalmist says, exuding gratitude, "What shall I render to the Lord for all that He has given me?" (Ps. 115:12).

I am a relatively young priest, one who does not possess the depth of wisdom or the breadth of experiences of my brother clergymen. At the same time, as we think about cultivating future priests to serve in Christ's vineyard, I hope a younger perspective is valuable. We need priests to continue bringing Christ's light and life to the world around us and I hope this reflection helps.

I graduated from Holy Cross Greek Orthodox School of Theology in May, 2019, and was ordained to the diaconate and priesthood the next month. It was a whirlwind of experiences and changes for my young family and me. While ordination was the beginning of the road as a clergyman, it was the end of a long, deliberate, and prayerful process during which I grappled intensely with whether I was called to ordained ministry.

I began considering the priesthood as a thirteen-year-old middle schooler, growing up at St. Nicholas in St. Louis, Missouri. Raised by faithful parents who always prioritized the church, I loved to serve as an acolyte. The experience of being in the holy altar on Sundays and around the Paschal season made an indelible impact on my life. That experience, combined with participating in other elements of parish life, led to my firmly held belief that being part of a parish committed to God and committed to something higher than our desires is invaluable.

Unlike some young men, however, I was not ready to make the leap into seminary immediately after high school.

Instead, I studied at the University of Missouri, where I prepared to enter law school. Of all the professions, I wanted most to be a lawyer (in spite of Luke 11:52,"Woe to you lawyers! For you have taken away the key of knowledge. You did not enter yourselves, and you hindered those who were entering."!) Throughout my time in college, I began reading more scripture and writings from the Church Fathers. I also increased my liturgical participation and was struck by the simple yet sweet community of St. Luke in Columbia, Missouri. My love for the Church grew and grew. In college I also spent my summers working with an Orthodox mission group and my desire to live a life of sacrifice in Christ was growing. Yet, despite all these blessings, I still waffled between attending seminary or applying to law school. I distinctly remember on multiple occasions packing away the LSAT books, only to retrieve these prep materials from my closet a week or two later.

Having taken the plunge and enrolling in seminary, the wrestling and struggling did not go away. I was taking the courses and doing the work of a man preparing for the priesthood, sure, but throughout my four years at Holy Cross, there were extended periods of time during which I seriously wondered whether this path was for me. Like Jacob wrestling the angel in the book of Genesis, I struggled and fought whether I was suited for ordained ministry. Serving as a priest brings indescribable joys, of course, but it also takes much fortitude, patience, and steadfastness, and I was not convinced I would be able to endure this kind of vocation for decades and decades.

There's much more that could be said. But in all these stages of doubt and contemplation, there were always wonderful priests present. I received good advice, yes, but most times the priests in my life did not disseminate wise counsel. They instead served as steady pillars, pillars who steadied a young man discerning his vocation. As the Ethiopian man says to the Apostle Philip in the Book of Acts, "How can I [understand] unless someone guides me?" (Acts 26:31). It is through the example, the devotion, and the love of these priests that I became willing to accept this calling. Partnered with an unflappable presvytera, who was willing to go anywhere to serve God, and the witness of the priests who surrounded me throughout life, allowed me to apply for ordination to the holy priesthood.

I will conclude this little reflection where I began. The Psalmist writes, "O Lord, how sweet are thy words to my taste, sweeter than honey to my mouth!" This exact sweetness, this experiential understanding of Christ and His Gospel struck me with an overwhelming desire to serve Christ and His Church that could not be dissuaded by lofty career prospects or high worldly status. It's my hope that during priestly ministry, I am found worthy to transmit our Lord Jesus Christ's sweetness to all people whom I encounter. Many, many people experience bitterness in their life. Some experience the totality of life as one giant helping of bitterness. The Church and her priests must serve as God's ambassadors bringing our Lord's sweet taste to those whom we encounter.

Father John Tsikalas serves
at Saint Andrew Church in South Bend, Indiana.

Deacon Vincent Benson

T he waters of the Mediterranean lapped against the sides of the little, open boat as we moved across the sea towards the Lérins islands, off the coast of France near Cannes. I was visiting my girlfriend, Pamela, who was studying in Avignon, France, and we had made a little trip to the Riviera. It was a beautiful place, and once we got to the islands, we wandered, enjoying the pine forests mixed with palm trees.

The islands have been inhabited since at least Roman times, and around the year 410, St Honoratus founded a monastery there, which persisted until the French Revolution. Many famous Gallic monks lived there; the most famous include St. Vincent of Lérins and, according to tradition, St Patrick of Ireland. In the aftermath of the revolution, Cistercians re-animated the monastery, which is still in operation today as a Roman Catholic monastery.

Pamela and I stood outside the monastery and prayed. For kids from wintry Minnesota, it was a celestial moment, standing there in the sand among the palm and pine trees, praying before such an old, holy place.

I was raised to love Jesus in a Lutheran home, and I love Him now. At some point, however, I began to have doubts about the way I was worshipping Him. After a lot of prayer, study, and anguish, I came to mistrust the wisdom of the Reformation. I arrived in a place where I knew I would either become Roman Catholic or Eastern Orthodox, the two churches from before the Reformation. I continued to study and visit churches.

The first time I visited an Orthodox Church, it was St Basil's day, and not only did I experience some strange (to me) worship, but I was there for the Vasilopita, which also seemed unusual, but pleasant. I continued to visit Roman Catholic Churches too, and to worship in my Lutheran church, but I yearned to get back to that Orthodox church—there was so much I didn't understand, and the place intrigued me.

I did return, and then more and more often. I continued to study church history too, but at some point, I realized that reading would only take me so far. I decided one fall that I wanted to try to live an "Orthodox life," as much as I could—so, attending all the worship services, fasting, daily prayer, and doing the best I could without the sacraments.

By the time I got through Great Lent and Pascha, I was eager to get in. My priest, Fr. Timothy Sas, had spent a lot of time talking to me and listening. He didn't want me to rush, but he agreed that I could be chrismated on May 24th (Holy Spirit Day that year).

Part of my chrismation involved having a saint. As I looked through the list on May 24th, I saw that one of the saints of that day was St Vincent of Lérins. Lérins sounded familiar, but I just couldn't remember why. When I looked it up, I realized with amazement that I had been to that island over 30 years earlier, and that my girlfriend (now my wife) and I had prayed there—I felt like St. Vincent had been looking after us all those years!

My Orthodox life has been a great blessing to me. So much of the advice that I encounter today has to do with "finding one's purpose," or "making one's own meaning." That's not all bad, but Orthodoxy has given me purpose and meaning that I didn't have to conjure up myself.

As I continued to live an Orthodox life—now with sacraments—I fell deeper and deeper in love with our worship. I never miss church if I can manage it. I became a chanter and struggled through the long and steep learning associated with that. I learned so much from those hymns!

Along the way, a young deacon, Fr. Dustin Lyon, spent some time at our church after seminary while he waited for a call. Once, he said to me, "You know, you could really help this church by being ordained a deacon." I hadn't thought of it, but it seemed unlikely. I had attended Divinity School as a young man; I felt now like I was running out of time to seek ordination to any role.

At some point, I talked with Fr. Timothy, and he encouraged me to think and pray about it. I learned that becoming a deacon wasn't the long, arduous graduate school process required to become a priest. I had also fallen in love with my church, and I thought that, as Fr. Dustin had suggested, I could help my brothers and sisters there by being ordained. That fall, I met with our bishop, and while it ended up being a long wait, I was ordained on April 1st, 2023, the day of St Mary of Egypt. I was ordained Vincent, so my beloved saint is even more on my mind and heart now.

Fr. Timothy had moved on to Minneapolis, but he was able to be there for my ordination, accompanying me on my Orthodox journey just as he has now for 17 years. Our new priest had been with us for just over a year—and he is Fr. Dustin Lyon, who had been away for ten years serving two other churches. Now he is reaping the result of his suggestion so many years before.

From the moment I asked Fr. Timothy about ordination, I continued to struggle with the decision. Even up to shortly before my ordination, I was wracked with uncertainty about what was best. In my case, the process took an unusually long time (ten years!), and I gave up inside a number of times; but God has His timing, and I trust that there was some purpose in all of that.

As it is, I love being a deacon. Even though the services are physically challenging for someone who is old and overweight, I look forward to them. Our Archdeacon, Fr. Vasilios Smith, once told me that, after a while, my diaconal service would become like a dance with my priest, and it's the truth (sometimes). I got to know some beautiful men in the diaconate program at Holy Cross, and I have come to love all of my brother clergy. It is so fun to get to know them and to serve at new places when I visit (sometimes a little terrifying too—but as I get more and more comfortable with my work, that part is getting better).

Just as rewarding are the ways in which I have been able to help the brothers and sisters I love here at Twelve Holy Apostles Church in Duluth. I was able to bring communion to one of my godsons, who was stricken with a serious medical condition. Recently, when Fr. Dustin was away, a sister entered the last day of her life. I brought her communion and prayed with her and her family and then visited them later in the day and after her repose. I am so grateful that I am ordained to do such things—it was a great blessing for me.

I thank God that He brought me home to Orthodoxy, and I pray that He brings many more to be blessed as I have been.

Deacon Vincent Benson serves at
Twelve Holy Apostles Church in Duluth, Minnesota.

Deacon Mark Bradshaw

Growing up as the child of Protestant ministers, I saw the Christian life from an early, unique vantage point. My parents dedicated themselves to the church and the needs of their congregation, embodying a devotion to faith both publicly and privately. This commitment to ministry was a family tradition; my uncle was also a Protestant pastor, my oldest sister and her husband serve as pastors, and several of my cousins have dedicated their lives to missionary work. On both my mother's and father's sides, my family held a deep belief in the value of serving the Christian community. I was deeply blessed by their example, as they instilled in me a desire to serve God and His people. However, I also witnessed the immense personal toll that full-time ministry exacted: the long hours, the weight of parishioners' struggles, and the sacrifices required to meet the community's needs. From an early age, I was determined that I would serve the church, but never as clergy; I wanted to be a faithful layperson, committed to my faith without bearing the burdens that clergy life had placed on my family.

In my adult years, my journey took me further from my Protestant roots and eventually led me to the Orthodox Church. This discovery of ancient Christianity felt, in many ways, like finding something both familiar and entirely new. The Orthodox Church, while far removed from my charismatic Protestant upbringing in some respects, also held profound similarities. One of the most striking aspects was the warmth and openness with which my family and I were welcomed into our local Orthodox parish. Though our parish was small, it quickly became a second family to us, and soon I found myself becoming deeply involved in parish life, including serving on the parish council and helping organize ministries.

Over time I came to see the unique liturgical and pastoral needs of our parish. Though I remained cautious about formal clerical roles, I felt a growing desire to help meet these needs. This internal pull intensified during the COVID pandemic. Our parish was affected significantly due to the health needs of our priest's family, which highlighted a need for additional liturgical and pastoral support. As I saw these needs, I felt compelled to consider a role I had once dismissed. In my discernment, I came to understand the distinct roles within the church: the priesthood and the diaconate. While the priest leads the sacramental life of the parish, the deacon embodies a unique call to serve. This role resonated with me, as I felt my own strengths and desires were best expressed through service to others.

There are many Orthodox parishes served by a lone priest, with no one else to assist in the performance and organization of liturgical life. This can be a heavy and lonely existence, especially in towns or cities where there are no other Orthodox parishes nearby. The diaconate allows the liturgical life of a parish to be more fully realized and can share the rather heavy load of the parish priest. When the priest and deacon serve together, each is able to perform his respective parts of the liturgy, freeing the priest to more fully live play his own role. This distinction also allows the people to see the unique ways the Holy Spirit works through different callings, fostering a greater sense of ownership and participation in the church's liturgical life. The deacon can help to visit the sick and elderly in their homes and hospitals, distributing the Eucharist and praying. The deacon can also help to carry forward the various outreach efforts of the parish to the parishioners and the wider community.

With the blessing of Metropolitan Nathanael of Chicago, I entered the diaconate training program, and after a period of study and preparation, I was ordained on October 12th, 2024. This decision was not taken lightly, especially with the demands of a full-time job, an already full life, and a large family with seven children. At times, the thought of adding these new responsibilities felt overwhelming. Nevertheless, I believe that each parish deserves the fullness of the church's ministry and that the Holy Spirit provides for the church through the service of bishops, priests, and deacons. I look forward to a day when every parish in America has both a priest and a deacon to fulfill its mission more completely. I believe that there are many men who, like me, share a desire for greater service. The need is great, and the Holy Spirit is calling. I pray that there are many others who are willing to share in the burden and the blessings of this service.

Now, as I begin this new journey, I carry the legacy of my upbringing and the lessons of my past, striving to serve my community with the same dedication I saw in my parents. I am grateful for the ways my background has prepared me for this calling and hopeful for the opportunity to contribute to the life of the church in this new way.

Deacon Mark Bradshaw serves at
Annunciation Greek Orthodox Church
in Decatur, Illinois.

Deacon Theodore Saclarides

I chose to pursue the diaconate, not because of a moment of divine inspiration or enlightenment, but rather because of the encouragement and motivation provided by my beloved clergy, based on something they had seen in me. About thirty years ago, Fr. George Scoulas of blessed memory, asked me to serve as a "black robe" in the altar, supervising the altar boys, cutting prosforos, boiling water, etc., and I did so for twenty years. Father Angelo Artemas of blessed memory told me about the diaconate program and suggested I apply. After weeks of spinning my wheels and procrastinating, he filled out the application for me and mailed it in. I was reluctant to apply initially because I didn't feel called, nor did I feel worthy.

My journey as a deacon has been an ongoing process; there has been constant change and evolution. I still worry about making mistakes, and the physical demands are significant. I am slowly arriving at the point where serving has become increasingly spiritual and not limited to just remembering my cues and responsibilities. My favorite moments are reading the Gospel and giving communion, especially to kids. My final answer as to why I am a deacon might not become evident until some point in the future when He makes it known to me.

I recall the conversation I had one day with His Eminence Metropolitan Nathanael, when he told me not to be nervous when I serve. I admitted to him that I was nervous. He asked if I was nervous when I did surgery, and I said no because I had to focus on saving people's lives. He told me that we were doing the very same thing in church so I shouldn't be nervous, just focused.

This conversation occurred in the middle of Divine Liturgy when I was holding his staff by the bishop's throne on the solea. He is inspiring and a true shepherd of the flock.

In contrast, my career in surgery and medicine felt like a calling from a very young age. I was an avid student of science and mathematics, and it just seemed like medicine was the only thing I should do. Of course, it doesn't hurt when your grandmother reads the coffee grounds in the bottom of her cup of Greek coffee and tells you at age eight that you will be a surgeon! I have studied a lot of science, and it is clear to me that science proves the existence of God rather than proving His absence. There is structure, uniformity, and reproducibility in the universe that reflects a master plan and organization. For example, the laws of physics (e.g. gravity, inertia, equal and opposite forces) apply to everywhere in the universe. All of life, animal and plant, is based on a genetic code that consists of sequences of only four nucleic acids, and it is how these molecules are sequenced that distinguishes one life form from another. Many genes are the same, whether we are human, an ape, a cat, or a banana. All matter on the planet earth is composed of elemental atoms, of which there are about a hundred different ones (e.g. iron, oxygen, hydrogen, carbon) and these elements share common structure and physical properties. Yet their organization is so predictable and precise that they can be described in fixed rows and columns on a single sheet of paper, not hundreds of pages. In my opinion, what I have described above is a reflection of a divine presence.

Despite all the science I have learned, I don't have answers for many things I have seen in medicine. For example, I don't have a good explanation why there has to be suffering. What is there to learn from a child being stricken with cancer? What is the lesson to be learned from a loved one's mental illness or suicide? I have come to learn that our God is a loving, benevolent God, and that there is an opportunity to grow in God's Grace through suffering, but some days it's hard to accept this without questioning.

I trust that my final days will be filled with service to God and my fellow humans. As to the question of what was my calling? Beats me—I'm still working on it.

Deacon Theodore Saclarides, MD serves at
Saints Peter and Paul Church in Glenview, Illinois.

Deacon Prochoros Sbarounis

I have always loved our church, our traditions, and the meanings of both. Everything done during the liturgy, every prayer spoken, defines who we are and what we believe. I cannot say that I had a singular moment when I knew that I would be joining the ranks of the clergy. My faith has been a part of me for as long as I can remember. When the Diaconate Program at Holy Cross Greek Orthodox School of Theology was suspended, you could say that faith and perseverance were needed to find a way to get the education needed to follow the path to ordination.

Even though both my parents had passed, my faith was a mirror of my mother's, so the education was easy. As a husband, it was more unusual, as my wife was a recent convert to Orthodoxy and was still learning the rich history of the Church. As a father, my children learned at an early age about my sense of faith; my decision was not a surprise to anyone in my family. It was not a struggle; I had a burning desire to serve.

I would not call the process an obstacle but rather a delay in starting or God's time. I had three young boys when I learned of the Diaconate Program at Holy Cross. My wife encouraged me to enroll in the program but asked me to wait until our oldest started high school in a few years. Her request was not unreasonable, so I waited until 2015. When the time came to enroll, I went through the process only to find that the program was suspended. I was told the suspension was indefinite, so I had to look for an alternative program. The Orthodox Church in America (OCA) offered a program at St. Macrina Orthodox Institute, and my application was accepted. I started what turned out to be a six-year program. After completing the program at the direction of His Eminence, Metropolitan Nathanael, I attended two virtual sessions at Holy Cross.

My advice to anyone considering ordination: pray, pray, and pray. Speak to your spiritual father. Speak to your family. Speak to those who have been through the program, ordained and non-ordained. Understand the program and its sacrifice of family time (classes on weekends, assignments, summers at the seminary). Be realistic. Learn about the role of the diaconate, the history, and the traditions of whom and how we serve.

Deacon Prochoros Sbarounis serves at
St Sophia Church in Elgin, Illinois.

Archdeacon Vasilios Smith

On a recent leadership retreat for the Metropolis of Chicago, I found myself reunited with a person who I met just three weeks prior on an arch-pastoral visit with Metropolitan Nathanael to one of the smaller communities of our metropolis. During that visit I met many wonderful people who shared with me their roles within the parish community and for some, their journeys to orthodoxy.

This person was not a cradle orthodox as I had originally thought when we first met, and so I asked her to tell me "her story". She went on to tell me how a series of events, seemingly random at first, had led to her meeting her future husband in New York City, becoming engaged, becoming orthodox, marrying and eventually moving to this small town in the Metropolis of Chicago had played out. As her story unfolded, the series of events became more and more beautiful and more and more unbelievable. That said, it was crystal clear to me how God had His gentle and guiding hand in her journey to orthodoxy and in her overall life.

Later that same day at lunch, she asked me to tell her my story and how I came to be the Archdeacon of the Metropolis of Chicago. Since my ordination to the diaconate over 25 years ago, I've told my story dozens and dozens of times; and yet, each time I've told my story, I always had the feeling of coming up short. I routinely struggled and could not clearly and fully verbalize my calling to ordained ministry. I never experienced that single "aha" moment in my life that others may have experienced, and I never felt like I did a very good job when trying to connect the dots. This time, however, something felt very different. As I told her the seemingly random series of my life's events that led me to my ordination, I saw for the first time and very clearly how the gentle and guiding hand of God had shaped me as a youth to a calling of service and ministry. Reflecting on her story as I told mine brought me clarity that I had never seen before. There was no doubt in my mind that God worked through her to reveal that clarity. As I said, my calling was not a single life-changing event, but one of countless events that changed and shaped me for over 45 years. Here's my story:

I was raised in a small furniture town in southwestern New York. From my earliest memories at the community of St. Nicholas in Jamestown, NY through high school graduation, we would see no fewer than five priests assigned to our community. My family grew close to all of the priests and their families over that period of time. It was something that just happened, and I never thought twice about it. We were active in all aspects of church life, and we would also spend considerable time with the priests and their families socially. For one priest and his presbytera, Jamestown was their very first assignment. They also started their family there. Another priest, an archimandrite, lost his presbytera when their 6 children were young and raised them with the help of his mother. The other priests assigned to Jamestown were in the midst of very successful and active ministries, one of them serving in Jamestown for over 20 years. From all the priests, both young and old, I learned and developed a deep love of liturgy. I saw first-hand how they sacrificed and served the community. They were humble priests, and they showed us that while they had a divine calling, they were approachable, relatable and down-to-earth.

Prior to leaving for the University of Detroit to continue my studies in chemical engineering, I spent the summer at the Ionian Village (IV) in Greece. My love of liturgy continued to grow at IV, as did my overall understanding of our faith and the importance of our saints, especially St. Dionysios and St. Nectarios.

While studying in Detroit, I was able to assist and travel with His Grace Bishop Timothy (Negropontis) and His Grace Bishop Iakovos (Garmatis), both of blessed memory. Many wonderful priests there continued to impact my spiritual life and my love for our Lord grew even stronger.

As my studies began in Detroit, I started having second thoughts about my career path and wondered about going to the seminary. Bishop Iakovos encouraged me to finish my degree and start my career. It was shortly after this conversation that I was introduced to my future bride by Bishop Timothy.

A year after I commenced my secular career at Dow Chemical Company, we were married, and some two years later, the first of four daughters was born. For over ten years we were part of the community of St. Demetrios in Saginaw, Michigan. I served in the altar there from day one and began contemplating ordained ministry. After transferring with Dow to Illinois, we moved to Aurora and joined the church of St. Athanasios. From much encouragement from then Bishop Iakovos of Chicago and continuous support and mentoring from our parish priest, Fr. Christopher Constantinides, I petitioned for ordination in 1995. My application was approved by Archbishop Iakovos in July 1996, and I was ordained to the diaconate on November 16, 1996. I was blessed to serve at St. Athanasios for several years and then, as specific needs arose around the Metropolis, I was assigned to many different parishes. Since completing the Diaconate Program in 2010 I have returned to Holy Cross Hellenic College for summer sessions to teach teleturgics and mentor new and aspiring deacons. I was elevated to Archdeacon by His Eminence Metropolitan Nathanael on December 9, 2018.

My life has been filled with so many blessings, and my calling to ordained ministry has never been more clear to me. Unworthy as I am, the gentle and guiding hand of God has brought me to where I am today. I pray that my story may be of some inspiration to others as they navigate their calling to serve God and His church in whatever capacity God wills.

Glory be to God!

Archdeacon Vasilios Smith
serves at the Metropolis of Chicago

Deacon Paul S. Speed

My journey to ordination started on a late summer evening a few months before my fifth birthday in August, likely, of 1962. My parents, involved in our (Baptist) church, were hosting a missionary who was staying with us while reporting back to the congregations that supported him, resting, and raising funds. After supper, I went in to help him unpack, or just to visit because there was this exotic person in our small house.

I know it was summer because the windows were open, the slanting western sun was coming through them, and the sounds of the neighborhood in our small town were audible. I know I was four, because we moved a couple hours away the next March, after I turned five in November.

The man asked me my name and I told him, "Scott," but also volunteered that my first name was Paul; for reasons I have never quite understood, my parents called me by my middle name. He stopped what he was doing, had me sit down, and told me all about my namesake,

St. Paul the Apostle. He then asked me to think about following the apostle's example in working for Christ.

He made a great impression on me, particularly because he took me seriously. Who takes a four-year-old seriously? He made me think about doing something formal for Christ, dedicating myself to him, something I considered on and off for the next fifty years. I wish I could remember his name.

Ten years later, and three towns later, I was in confirmation classes. Our pastor was a converted Roman Catholic who took church history very seriously and taught it well. He encouraged us all to pray about our vocations and charged us to take our faith seriously. Years later, I would realize this was the first I even heard of the Orthodox faith; my small rural county was not very diverse ethnically or as to faith.

In college, I became more interested in the church and took on a theology minor. One of our professors, who eventually moved on to teach at an Episcopal seminary, asked me if I had considered exploring ordination. I was surprised; at the time I was planning to be the next great classical composer. I respected him and began thinking again about my calling, and this time, about seeking ordination.

My fiancée (now wife) and I joined the Episcopal Church about this time, and I began the process of discernment about seeking ordination. In our Lord's great providence, I did not get far in the process at that time; I would have made myself and some poor parish quite miserable had I been ordained at that time.

Ten years later, following marriage, the birth of our first two children, and a near-fatal auto accident, I was encouraged to consider entering the ordination discernment process again. For quite mundane reasons, that didn't happen.

Fast forward ten or so years; we had been chrismated into the Orthodox Church in 1992. Life had intervened; I had spent ten years in the newspaper business and was just a year into my career in state service. There was a lot to absorb for two non-Greek protestants and their three children (soon to be four) in a parish that was, at that time, substantially Greek.

We had not set out to be Greek Orthodox, only to be Orthodox. There were two Orthodox parishes in our area, both fifty miles away. A parishioner at St. George in Rock Island, Ted Vlahos, may his memory be eternal, invited our Episcopal priest to the epitaphio service. They were friends at the local coffee hangout. Father Marshall did not want to drive the hour alone, so I went with him.

It felt like home. The story of our conversion was also marked with people who nudged us in the right direction, people who did not know each other and who often had no idea we were looking.

Our warm reception planted a seed, or rather revived a seed planted many years before. I wanted to explore a formal way of serving the parish that had so taken us into its heart. A friend from our Episcopal days had been chrismated into a parish in the western suburbs of Chicago and had been encouraged to enter the St. Stephen's Course, a program of the Antiochian Archdiocese. He was subsequently ordained to the diaconate and the priesthood.

It was around 2001, and a couple of people in the parish, St. George in Rock Island, suggested I might seek ordination as a deacon. We explored and found out there was not such a program in the Greek church, so I ended up doing the Antiochian program, with no idea of ordination. After all, if you ask for God's will and the answer seems to be no, you take it.

The Antiochian program also offered a master's program at that time, through the University of Balamand. I received much encouragement and support from members of the parish and completed that course and then the master's degree.

As this process continued, I was encouraged by Fr. Dean Photos and Fr. Leo Gavrilos to continue in my studies. Father Leo helped by getting me in touch with the Metropolis of Chicago, as the diaconate program at Holy Cross had started by then. The number of parishioners who encouraged me and helped me and supported along the way is large, and for fear of omitting someone I won't name them.

Finally, with the help of Fr. Christodolous Margellos, my spiritual father, I was accepted to the Holy Cross Diaconate Program and completed it in 2011. In December of 2012, under the omophorion of Metropolitan Iakovos of blessed memory, I was ordained to the diaconate. His Grace Bishop Demetrios of Mokissos helped greatly; he was very patient as he walked me through the paperwork and procedures leading up to this pivotal moment.

Since then, I have served the parish of St. George, for the last several years under Fr. Michael Constantinides. He has encouraged me and given me more responsibilities, especially after my retirement from the Department of Corrections in 2017.

I did not have a road-to-Damascus moment. My path to holy orders started as a child and was a winding path that took me through three protestant groups before leading me to Orthodoxy; there were several roadblocks and detours. Several times it seemed like the least likely outcome for my life, and yet there would be an encouraging person, a priest, pastor, or parishioner.

In my professional life, when I have needed a new job, I realized it only because it opened, and someone suggested it. Perhaps I am not the most sensitive of people to the Lord's leading; I need to be reminded again and again. Did my call start at age four, to be answered at age fifty-five?

That is how it looks from here.

I would be remiss in not mentioning the support of my wife, who put up with my doing course work, chant classes, and evening services while she raised four children. My in-laws supported us as well, even when I took their first born and their four grandchildren into a church they didn't really understand.

I started, fitfully, to seek the Lord's will when I was four; It took me fifty years to learn to seek His will consistently. Most people, I suspect, are a little quicker to pick up on the clues.

Deacon Paul Speed serves at
Saint George Church in Rock Island, Illinois.

Deacon Luke Twito

W hen I was about twelve years old, I asked my father for advice on what I should do with my life. He answered, "You have God-given abilities, and you have God-given responsibilities.

Whatever you choose to do, do your best." My father was a Marine Corps pilot, who also chose a career in commercial aviation. My mother served in WWII as a WASP (Women Airforce Service Pilot). They each loved flying. I began to plan for the possibility of becoming a pilot, but also felt that medicine might ultimately be my career path. When I was thirteen, our family went through the trauma of losing my older sister in a car accident. She had felt a calling to serve God in Africa as a medical missionary. One morning, coming home from working the late-night shift as a nurse, she fell asleep at the wheel and was killed instantly when her car struck a bridge abutment. Life for me became more intentional. From that moment, I was determined to never add to my parents suffering through disobedience or recklessness.

My life decisions began to be considered through various lenses: Will this activity help make me a better doctor? How can I lead my life to someday have an excellent marriage? Where can I experience God in a profound way and have my faith strengthened? As an example, when my mother asked if I would like to spend some of my summer at a relative's farm in Iowa, I said, "Yes." I thought since I was born and raised in Minneapolis and knew nothing about small towns, let alone life on a farm, it would help me relate to more people eventually as their doctor.

I took flight lessons and soloed a single engine Cessna at age sixteen. Prior to that I had to have a physical examination which I obtained from my father's flight surgeon. He had heard that I was interested in medicine and offered to have me watch one of his surgeries. That day was life- changing in that I witnessed my first surgery and now had a role model and mentor to guide me. My training was rigorous and consumed the next fifteen years after high school. My career spanned another thirty years as an orthopedic surgeon. God was with me every step of the way. I witnessed miracles. It was, I believe, my first calling.

My religious life began in the Lutheran church where I was baptized and confirmed. I sang in the church choir and served as an acolyte. Looking back, I am grateful for my parents' example and faithfulness in bringing us to church on a regular basis. Yet, despite all the years spent in Sunday school and at my Christian grade school, it was in high school that I recall struggling with the question, "Am I saved?" Once I left home for college, I became involved in various Bible study and religious fellowship groups, pursuing God not only as my Savior, but also as Lord of my life.

My cradle Orthodox wife, Mary Kay, and I met while I was in my second year in medical school. I knew in my heart that God had prepared each of us uniquely to be together in marriage. We did premarital counseling at St. Mary's Greek Orthodox Church and were married there in 1981.

God provided me with excellent role-models and guides on my path towards eventually joining the Church through chrismation in 1990.

It was during my years as a pilgrim and confirmand preparing to enter the Church, that I was asked to address a clergy group on the topic of healing. I was the new orthopedic surgeon in the town of Albert Lea, Minnesota. They were the "Southeastern Minnesota

Clergy Association" and comprised of approximately forty pastors and priests. After I had finished touching on the connections of physical, psychological, and spiritual healing, I asked for questions. The first question was, "How do you fight burnout?" I sensed that what they really meant to say was, "How can we fight burnout?"

I had always assumed that other people might burn out, but certainly not clergy. I replied with something like, "I have heard it said that we should assume that every conversation and what may appear to be chance introductions were arranged by God. So, when you visit someone in the hospital, you must feel on fire. God may have prepared that moment for you to bring a message that could have eternal significance." One person immediately responded, "You would think that." He went on to explain that for some of them, a hospital can be a challenging environment. As I listened and reflected, I believe God placed a calling in my heart—a calling, after a career in medicine, to serve the Church and assist the clergy especially in the area of hospital visits and other medically-related ministries.

Over the last thirty years, I have felt nothing but support from the priests who have served at St. Mary's. They welcomed me into the altar and saw to it that early on I was tonsured a reader.

Twenty years ago, two of them went with me to seek the blessing of Bishop Iakovos in Chicago for me to someday begin formal studies towards ordination as a deacon. I retired from my career in orthopedic surgery at the beginning of 2018. That summer I traveled to Iveron Monastery on Mount Athos, eager to tell Fr. Leondios, one of the monks, about my plans to apply to Holy Cross Greek Orthodox School of Theology and begin studies for the diaconate. He stopped me in my tracks with the question, "What does your wife think?" I assumed she was onboard with the decision since I had discussed with so many people what I felt was a calling to serve the Church in this capacity. He reminded me that her life and our family would be affected by this decision. Returning home, I was anxious to discuss with my wife her feelings about my seeking ordination and then truly receive her blessing and commitment to join me in this service to the Church. I completed the diaconate program at the end of 2020 and was ordained a deacon on June 18th, 2022.

My brother candidates and deacons that I have met each have unique stories to share about their backgrounds and callings. One can only marvel at how God's plan is working itself out in each of their lives. As my own ordination drew closer, I asked my priest, Fr. Timothy Sas, about how one can know if their calling to ordained ministry is authentic. He answered that the calling is placed in your heart by the Holy Spirit, that by God's grace you have the ability to do that which you are called to do, and that the calling is validated by your local community and the Church through the office of the bishop. I believe that a spiritual father is initially indispensable in helping someone ascertain God's call to ordained ministry. Later, his prayers, Godly wisdom, and guidance are critical to protecting the newly ordained. In the last four years I have experienced spiritual warfare and been tested far more than at any other time in my life. At ordination the grace of the Holy Spirit is called down to complete in us what is lacking, to preserve us, and to make us worthy to serve and to please God in the office which He has bestowed on us.

May we remember to pray for all those in ordained ministry that God continue to protect, sustain, and bless them and their families. May He bring us all to salvation. Glory to God.

Deacon Luke Twito MD serves at
Saint Mary's Church in Minneapolis, Minnesota.

AFTERWORD

THE BEAUTY OF UNIQUE CALLINGS

As the pages of this book reveal, the journey to ordained ministry is not a uniform path but a deeply personal and sacred pilgrimage. Each story within this collection bears witness to the truth that God calls His servants in profoundly unique and individual ways. From childhood moments of awe to life-altering experiences later in life, these narratives show that there is no singular formula for discerning the call to serve the Lord in ordained ministry.

This diversity reflects the boundless creativity of our Creator, who equips each of us with distinct gifts, talents, and experiences. While we are united in the shared mission to serve Christ and His Church, we are not all called to the same type of ordained ministry. Some are called to the holy diaconate, serving as Christ's hands in works of charity, humility, and liturgical assistance. Others are called to the priesthood, standing at the altar to offer the Holy Mysteries and shepherd their flock with love and wisdom. And still others are called to the episcopacy, bearing the weight of oversight and guiding the faithful with apostolic grace.

Even within each rank of ordained ministry, the call to serve takes on countless forms. A deacon may be especially gifted in outreach to the poor; a priest may be a profound teacher of the faith; a hierarch may be called to forge bonds of unity across communities. God's call is never generic; it is deeply personal, woven into the fabric of our lives and aligned with the gifts He has entrusted to us.

It is my fervent hope that this first volume will achieve its purpose: to strengthen the fraternal bonds among the clergy of the Holy Metropolis of Chicago and to inspire future generations of men who are pondering their calling to ordained ministry. May the heartfelt stories contained within these pages encourage those discerning their own path to see that no two callings are the same and that God's providence is always at work, gently leading each of us toward Him.

This volume is only the beginning of a greater journey. The subsequent books in this series will explore the callings of the laity—those called to serve Christ and His Church through parish ministries and through their careers. It is my hope that these future volumes will help all the faithful discern their calling to serve God and their neighbor, whether by participating in the life of their parish or by living out their faith in their workplaces, homes, and communities. The words of the Lord Jesus Christ Himself remind us of the sacred duty to serve one another:

> For I was hungry and you gave me food, I was thirsty and you gave me drink, I was a stranger and you took me in, I was naked and you clothed me, I was sick and you visited me, I was in prison and you came to me... Assuredly, I say to you, inasmuch as you did it to one of the least of these my brethren, you did it to me
>
> (Matt. 25:35-36, 40).

True service to God is inseparable from service to our neighbor. Whether in the sanctuary, the parish hall, or the workplace, each of us is given opportunities to embody Christ's love through our actions. Saint John Chrysostom reinforces this truth, reminding us that all Christians—clergy and laity alike—are called to live lives of service:

Do you wish to honor the body of Christ? Do not ignore Him when He is naked. Do not pay Him homage in the temple clad in silk, only to neglect Him outside where He suffers cold and nakedness. He who said:

> 'This is My Body,' is the same who said: 'You saw me hungry and you gave me no food,' and 'Whatever you did to the least of my brothers, you did also to me...' Honor Him, then, by sharing your wealth with the poor
>
> (Homily 50 on Matthew).

As we reflect on these narratives and look ahead to what lies beyond, let us remember that God's call to serve is both an invitation and a gift. It requires of us humility, prayer, and the courage to say, "Here I am, Lord. Send me." Whether we are called to serve as deacons, priests, hierarchs, or faithful laity, our lives gain purpose when we respond to His voice with trust and love.

May this series inspire all who read it to discern their own calling and embrace the unique ways they are invited to serve God and neighbor. May it foster a deeper sense of gratitude for the diversity of ministries within the Church and a renewed commitment to the work of the Gospel.

To Him who calls us, equips us, and sustains us in our service, be glory, honor, and worship, now and forevermore.

+NATHANAEL
Metropolitan of Chicago

www.ingramcontent.com/pod-product-compliance
Lightning Source LLC
Chambersburg PA
CBHW070121100426
42744CB00010B/1885